Contents

Understanding the revised Early Years Foundation Stage

The revised Statutory Framework for the Early Years Foundation Stage spells out the standards and requirements which govern all early years provision in England from September 2012. It can be downloaded from www.education.gov.uk or www.foundationyears.org.uk. The Statutory Framework is also included as an appendix to this resource.

The statutory document lists requirements for early years settings as they support children's **learning and development**, and **safeguarding and welfare**. As a brief legal document, it outlines areas of practice in straightforward terms but does not attempt to reflect the complex thinking and deeper understanding that early years practitioners draw on in order to provide high quality services to young children and families.

This resource can be used as a supplement to the Statutory Framework, and will support early years practitioners to consider some of the implications of the requirements by relating the framework to their own beliefs and practices in their setting. It works as a 'read-along guide' by providing additional explanation linked to sections of the Framework, as well as giving links to the wealth of further existing practice guidance.

The *Statutory Framework for the Early Years Foundation Stage (2012)* is referenced throughout this resource as **SF** and the *'Development Matters is the Early Years Foundation Stage'* non-statutory guidance is referenced as **DM**.

1

Introduction

> Every child deserves the best possible start in life and the support that enables them to fulfil their potential. Children develop quickly in the early years and a child's experiences between birth and age five have a major impact on their future life chances. A secure, safe and happy childhood is important in its own right. Good parenting and high quality early learning together provide the foundation children need to make the most of their abilities and talents as they grow up.
>
> **Statutory Framework for the Early Years Foundation Stage (I)**

This opening statement in the revised EYFS statutory document establishes some core ideas which underpin the mandatory framework. They could be expressed simply like this:

- **Every child matters**.
- **Children are both *being* and *becoming*** – children have a right to a happy childhood, and their early experiences lead to their development in ways that affect their future life chances.
- **Parents are the most important** support for children's development. High quality early learning in settings is most effective in partnership with parents.

As well as focussing on children's learning and development, health and safety, the EYFS promotes 'school readiness' as an objective of early years practice (SF II). This phrase does not sit well with many early years practitioners, since it seems to ignore the need to provide rich opportunities for children to develop in their unique ways, and the value of early childhood and early education for its own sake. Instead, it seems to hold up the beginning of statutory schooling as an established 'one-size-fits-all' gateway to future life, which children must be moulded in to. We would however, argue that excellent early years practice, which strives to understand and meet the needs of each child, is the best way to help children progress. Early years practice starts with the child, not with the curriculum.

Instead of looking at a 'one-size-fits-all' definition of school readiness, it might be helpful to think more broadly about the 'becoming' aspect of childhood. We know optimal early years experiences give a powerful boost to children as they continue to grow and learn beyond their earliest years. The Statutory Framework describes 'the broad range of knowledge and skills that provide the right foundation for good future progress through school and life', and 'the foundation children need to make the most of their abilities and talents as they grow up'. We know that this foundation is not limited to a narrow set of specific skills, but rests on other factors that will support the child through their lifetime:

- emotional well-being, based in close and warm relationships,
- confident and creative engagement with the world and other people developed through play in enabling outdoor and indoor environments, and
- independent thought and the ability to take responsibility and manage circumstances, based in experiences of making choices and being supported to become independent.

The EYFS charges practitioners to support children toward their successful futures, and we can reflect on how that is accomplished through being supportive partners for each child in their present moment. We value both who individual children are and where they are in their learning and development, and we also ensure that doors are open to new experiences and opportunities that will help them to progress.

Themes and principles

**The EYFS is based on four themes and the principles which inform them (SF VI).
They are:**

Themes	A Unique Child	Positive Relationships	Enabling Environments	Learning and Development
Principles	Every child is a unique child who is constantly learning and can be resilient, capable, confident and self-assured.	Children learn to be strong and independent through positive relationships.	Children learn and develop well in enabling environments, in which their experiences respond to their individual needs and there is a strong partnership between practitioners and parents and carers.	Children develop and learn in different ways. The framework covers the education and care of all children in early years provision, including children with special educational needs and disabilities.

These themes and principles help guide early years practice by putting a strong spotlight on core messages.

They are useful in
- reviewing our priorities and practice, and
- communicating clearly with colleagues and parents about how we work together to support children.

The themes are interrelated, and together explain how early years settings support children.

A Unique Child + **Positive Relationships** + **Enabling Environments** = **Learning and Development**

A Unique Child actively drives their own learning, reaching out and making sense of their experiences with people and the world around them. Within warm and loving **Positive Relationships** the child experiences emotional safety which is the bedrock to learning about how to be a person, and becomes a social learner interacting with others and learning from others. **Enabling Environments** provide the stimulating outdoor and indoor experiences – in settings and at home – which challenge children, respond to their interests and meet their needs. The result of these three elements interacting together is the child's **Learning and Development**.

The Early Years Foundation Stage: Themes and Commitments

A Unique Child

1.1 Child Development
Babies and children develop in individual ways and at varying rates. Every area of development – physical, cognitive, linguistic, spiritual, social and emotional – is equally important.

1.2 Inclusive Practice
The diversity of individuals and communities is valued and respected. No child or family is discriminated against.

1.3 Keeping Safe
Young children are vulnerable. They develop resilience when their physical and psychological well-being is protected by adults.

1.4 Health and Well-being
Children's health is an integral part of their emotional, mental, social, environmental and spiritual well-being and is supported by attention to these aspects.

Positive Relationships

2.1 Respecting Each Other
Every interaction is based on caring professional relationships and respectful acknowledgement of the feelings of children and their families.

2.2 Parents as Partners
Parents are children's first and most enduring educators. When parents and practitioners work together in early years settings, the results have a positive impact on children's development and learning.

2.3 Supporting Learning
Warm, trusting relationships with knowledgeable adults support children's learning more effectively than any amount of resources.

2.4 Key Person
A key person has special responsibilities for working with a small number of children, giving them the reassurance to feel safe and cared for and building relationships with their parents.

Enabling Environments

3.1 Observation, Assessment and Planning
Babies and young children are individuals first, each with a unique profile of abilities. Schedules and routines should flow with the child's needs. All planning starts with observing children in order to understand and consider their current interests, development and learning.

3.2 Supporting Every Child
The environment supports every child's learning through planned experiences and activities that are challenging but achievable.

3.3 The Learning Environment
A rich and varied environment supports children's learning and development. It gives them the confidence to explore and learn in secure and safe, yet challenging, indoor and outdoor spaces.

3.4 The Wider Context
Working in partnership with other settings, other professionals and with individuals and groups in the community supports children's development and progress towards the outcomes of Every Child Matters: being healthy, staying safe, enjoying and achieving, making a positive contribution and economic well-being.

Learning and Development

4.1 Play and Exploration
Children's play reflects their wide ranging and varied interests and preoccupations. In their play children learn at their highest level. Play with peers is important for children's development.

4.2 Active Learning
Children learn best through physical and mental challenges. Active learning involves other people, objects, ideas and events that engage and involve children for sustained periods.

4.3 Creativity and Critical Thinking
When children have opportunities to play with ideas in different situations and with a variety of resources, they discover connections and come to new and better understandings and ways of doing things. Adult support in this process enhances their ability to think critically and ask questions.

4.4 Areas of Learning and Development
The Early Years Foundation Stage (EYFS) is made up of six areas of Learning and Development. All areas of Learning and Development are connected to one another and are equally important. All areas of Learning and Development are underpinned by the Principles of the EYFS.

00012-2007DOM-EN © Crown copyright 2007

ISBN 978-1-84478-886-6

department for
education and skills

Principles into practice

Keeping the themes and principles in mind is a useful place to start, but it is what we actually do in practice that counts. The **EYFS Commitments** spell out what we see in practice in effective early years settings, where practitioners are **committed to acting** in ways which uphold the principles.

The chart on page 7 is part of the set of EYFS (2008) non-statutory materials. The EYFS is not merely the Statutory Framework. Instead its real character and depth is described in the Practice Guidance, Principles into Practice cards, and further information on the original CD-ROM, as well as numerous guidance materials issued subsequently. These original practice guidance materials are still relevant, and have not been replaced. Only the Development Matters section of the Practice Guidance has been replaced, in order to align with the revised areas of learning in the EYFS (2012). **This can be downloaded from www.early-education.org.uk or www.foundationyears.org.uk**

Each of the Commitments is supported by a Principles into Practice card, which includes:

- Information on important **aspects** of the commitment

- **Effective practice** notes on what the commitment looks like in practice

- **Challenges and dilemmas** highlighted to deepen understanding of some of the situations practitioners may face in settings

- **Reflecting on practice** scenarios to spark thought and discussion about what this commitment means in individual settings.

What do these principles look like in practice?

There are almost as many answers to this as there are settings. Just as each child is a unique child, each setting is also a unique setting. Every setting has unique families, unique communities, unique premises and resources, and unique members of the early years team. A daily routine in a childminder's home with an age range of children from six months to six years would be quite different from in a large nursery group of three-year-olds, some of whom stay for half a day while others are there all day. A small rural pack-away setting will organise its environment differently from a children's centre with dedicated premises. Since approaches that work in one situation may not be appropriate in another, it would be impossible to prescribe exactly what the most effective practice would look like in every case.

What is important is for settings to consider the Commitments – general statements about what we know to be important in effective provision – in the light of their own circumstances. Instead of looking for a recipe to be followed, settings can think about what they are already doing within each of the commitments, and consider where there is room to develop and what changes are the right ones for them. This reflective practice calls on practitioners to

- reflect on what is important for the children and families they work with

- analyse their own practice

- evaluate effectiveness

- be creative in finding their own solutions to challenges.

In this way settings move beyond reading the Statutory Framework as if it will enable them to simply implement a set of instructions, and the result is much more confident and effective practice.

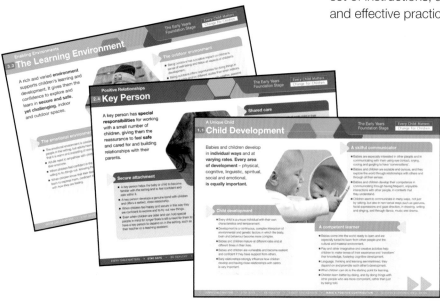

Learning and Development

The learning and development requirements within the Statutory Framework cover the **areas of learning and development**, the **early learning goals** for each area, and the **assessment requirements**. In addition, the document includes some descriptions of what providers must do within their practice, such as providing for learning through play, establishing an appropriate balance of child-initiated and adult-led activity, providing a key person system and working in partnership with parents and others. Each of these requirements is considered below.

The learning and development requirements apply to all providers except 'wrap around and holiday providers'. Wrap around provision is defined as 'Care offered before and after a school day e.g. by an after school club or by a childminder'. Holiday provision occurs 'exclusively in the school holidays'.

> Wrap around and holiday providers should be guided by, but do not necessarily need to meet, all the learning and development requirements. Practitioners should discuss with parents and/ or carers (and other practitioners and providers as appropriate) the support they intend to offer, seeking to complement learning in settings in which children spend more time.
>
> **Statutory Framework for the Early Years Foundation Stage 1.3**

2

Characteristics of effective teaching and learning

> In planning and guiding children's activities, practitioners must reflect on the different ways that children learn and reflect these in their practice. Three characteristics of effective teaching and learning are:
> * playing and exploring - children investigate and experience things, and 'have a go';
> * active learning - children concentrate and keep on trying if they encounter difficulties, and enjoy achievements; and
> * creating and thinking critically - children have and develop their own ideas, make links between ideas, and develop strategies for doing things.
>
> **Statutory Framework for the Early Years Foundation Stage 1.10**

It would be easy to miss the importance of the brief statement above. The characteristics of effective teaching and learning are given only this summary description in the statutory document, along with a requirement for the end-of-EYFS assessment (the EYFS Profile) of each child to include a short commentary on these (SF 2.8).

This slight mention, however, forms a bridge to the Commitments to support learning and development through **play and exploration**, **active learning**, and **creativity and critical thinking** – and makes it now mandatory for practitioners to respond not just to **what** children learn, but also to **how** they learn.

Of course these ideas about how children learn are not new. They reflect a long tradition of basing early years practice on play and rich hands-on experiences for young children, where children have choice and control over their learning. Respect for children as active, playful learners can seem at odds with the idea of early learning goals, raising concern that the EYFS is overly prescriptive in setting out expectations of what children will learn. Perhaps this new requirement to pay attention to how children learn will help to redress the balance, and reinforce practitioners' confidence to build on children's natural interests, motivations and strategies for learning.

This is also an invitation to explore these ideas more deeply, and to consider the latest evidence about why they are critical for children becoming effective learners and citizens for life. The next step from there is to reflect on and further develop the role of adults in fostering these ways of learning, helping children to remain powerful learners through the enabling environment of a setting and within interactions and relationships. **Further guidance on reflecting the characteristics of effective learning in practice can be found in *Development Matters in the Early Years Foundation Stage (EYFS)* (download from www.foundationyears.org.uk or www.early-education.org.uk)**

Learners for life

Recent research in brain development and psychology provides evidence of the remarkable learning abilities of babies and young children. Instead of needing months and years to develop as effective learners, from the very beginning children have strong drives to engage in the world and with other people, to become competent, and to make sense of their experiences. A young baby shows curiosity, makes choices and shows perseverance in reaching a goal. The youngest children are able to use most of the same strategies that will support them as learners all their lives, such as finding patterns in their experience so they can predict what will happen, and learning through imitating others.

Research is also demonstrating that these characteristics can be strengthened or hampered by the experiences children meet. When they are encouraged and supported to follow their curiosity, to feel the satisfaction of meeting their own challenges, to think for themselves, and to plan and monitor how they will go about their activities, they become self-regulated learners who later outstrip children who may have developed more early subject-based knowledge but are more passive in their learning.

Playing and exploring

This strand of the characteristics of effective learning begins to uncover why play is such a powerful arena for young children's learning. The three characteristics interact with each other, and play is one of the best opportunities for children to develop all the characteristics of effective learning – to be actively involved and motivated in their activities, as well as to think creatively and critically.

Playing and exploring can be considered in more detail like this:

Playing and exploring – engagement
Finding out and exploring   • **Showing curiosity about objects, events and people**   • **Using senses to explore the world around them**   • **Engaging in open-ended activity**   • **Showing particular interests**
Playing with what they know   • **Pretending objects are things from their experience**   • **Representing their experiences in play**   • **Taking on a role in their play**   • **Acting out experiences with other people**
Being willing to 'have a go'   • **Initiating activities**   • **Seeking challenge**   • **Showing a 'can do' attitude**   • **Taking a risk, engaging in new experiences, and learning from failures**

Finding out and exploring

The learning power of children finding out and exploring for themselves is clear to anyone who understands young children. Sensory exploration provides the raw data that children need in order to begin to understand their world.

Understanding the importance of multi-sensory experiences may support practitioners who work with babies and toddlers to assess, for instance, how enabling their environment is. Do the youngest children have opportunities outdoors to feel, see and hear the effect of the wind as it ruffles the leaves on a tree, or experience a hot sunny day and a drizzly rain? Can they see the light changing and the temperature drop as the sun moves behind a cloud? Indoors are they surrounded by mostly plastic and fluffy toys, or do they have opportunities to explore a range of everyday natural objects, materials, textures, and smells, and do you plan careful changes to what they can experience so that it sparks their interest and curiosity?

The aspect of open-ended sensory exploration is sometimes neglected as children mature. We don't leave exploring with our senses behind as we become able to use language and more abstract ways of learning. We still need to use all our senses when encountering new things. Having opportunities to explore materials freely before being asked to use them supports children to use new materials more effectively.

Playing with what they know

This element of play unaccountably doesn't appear in the statutory framework document, even though it is of fundamental importance to understanding why learning through play is at the core of early years practice. Even though policy makers may not understand why **playing around with ideas** is so important, early years practitioners need to place high priority here. It does appear in the *Development Matters in the Early Years Foundation Stage (EYFS)* document.

'Playing with what they know' refers to the imaginative side of play, where children enter the world of pretending. In their play children take what they know and begin to represent it in different ways.

Pretend play marks a move to a special kind of thinking, where children make one thing stand for something else in their minds – so the toy cow stands for a real cow, who moos and eats pretend 'grass' on the carpet. Next time the carpet may become a runway for an aeroplane. This ability to use objects to represent something else that they know about gives children flexibility in their minds, so that they can move beyond the here and now, to think about multiple possibilities. It helps them to look at the world and ask themselves, 'What if..?' and to think of possible answers. This is an important root of logic and abstract thought.

When children take on a role in their play, they are also becoming better learners because they are finding out about how people think – that the mummy has a different point of view from the baby, that the monster has a different idea from the super-hero. Becoming more aware of minds and thinking helps them to begin to understand and control their own thinking. They also get practice in self-control, because pretend play has built-in 'rules' that children follow in their play. You hold a wooden brick to your ear, for instance, when you are pretending it is a mobile phone. You would not put it in the fridge or pretend to eat it.

When children move into pretending along with other children, they develop more complex play that challenges them to negotiate roles and storylines, and to use their minds to solve the many problems that the play throws up.

Being willing to 'have a go'

The more experiences children have, the more they can learn. Children have an inborn drive to explore, but sometimes this can be dampened by circumstances. Children are more likely to welcome new experiences when they are encouraged to try things out, are supported in what they are trying to do, and know that what they do has an effect on the world around them. They enjoy challenges, and have a 'can-do' attitude. They take a risk with things that they are unsure about and aren't afraid to play around and experiment, because they know they can learn by trial and error.

Emotional safety is important here, since children are more independent in their activities when they know they have a safe base to return to, and won't be criticised when unexpected things happen. It's also important that the environment encourages children to have a go, with interesting things that children can explore, change and use in their own ways. A child passively watching television gets no response from the people and things on the screen, and becomes less sure about having a go in the world. But a child who can make lots of choices and see that their actions have an effect will know they are competent and will be keen to carry on interacting.

Active learning

Children are not waiting to be taught, but are energetic and active agents of their own learning and development. A good learner has a strong motivation, and enjoys mental and physical challenges on the way to reaching the goals they have set for themselves.

Active learning – motivation

Being involved and concentrating

- **Maintaining focus on their activity for a period of time**
- **Showing high levels of energy and fascination**
- **Not easily distracted**
- **Paying attention to details**

Keeping on trying

- **Persisting with activity when challenges occur**
- **Showing a belief that more effort or a different approach will pay off**
- **Bouncing back after difficulties**

Enjoying achieving what they set out to do

- **Showing satisfaction in meeting their own goals**
- **Being proud of how they accomplished something – not just the end result**
- **Enjoying meeting challenges for their own sake rather than external rewards or praise**

Being involved and concentrating

Children learn at a deep level when they are paying close attention and stretching their mental capacities to the full by being deeply involved in activities. You can recognise this kind of involvement when something captures a child's focussed attention so that they ignore distractions and become completely engrossed in enjoyment of the activity for its own sake.

Children gradually develop the ability to purposefully control and direct their attention. At any age, deep concentration and focussed attention can occur when something captures the child's interest. Curiosity is fuelled by the child's own drive to explore and understand the world, and so it is deeply enjoyable and satisfying to follow that desire. The more children have opportunities to become deeply involved, the more they will look for the satisfaction that comes from those experiences.

Children are more likely to become deeply involved in activities which they have chosen for themselves. Adults can ensure there are novel and stimulating resources and opportunities, based on children's interests, and that children can make their own choices about using these to satisfy their own curiosity. The enabling environment will also support children to concentrate by reducing unnecessary noise and providing visually calm areas, as well as by giving uninterrupted stretches of time where children can continue their activities to their natural conclusion.

The outdoor environment is an important part of active learning. Children who may drift from one activity to another indoors sometimes become energetically involved and show greater focus in their activities when they have the space and feeling of freedom they can experience outdoors.

Keeping on trying

Being able to stick with challenging situations is important in order to succeed in learning, and in life. Whether a child perseveres or gives up is a tendency that is developed early in life. The habit of trying hard and putting in continued effort in the face of difficulty grows when children have learned that their efforts obtain results.

Children need opportunities to do things for themselves, with just enough support and encouragement for them to discover that they can be successful. If there is too much help children don't have sufficient experience of challenge to learn how to handle it. On the other hand, there are times when a bit of help can enable a child to succeed at what they were trying to do, and encourage them that the satisfaction of success is worth the effort rather than giving up too quickly. Adults need to judge how to help children to succeed, without taking over from the child.

Enjoying achieving what they set out to do

When children complete an activity they have decided on or master a challenge they have set for themselves, they are being motivated from within. Research shows that this intrinsic motivation – striving to reach your own goals – leads to better learning, more enjoyment and greater success in activities than when you do something for an outside reward.

The Statutory Framework refers simply to children who 'enjoy achievements', but it is important to focus on supporting children to enjoy achieving their own goals, rather than relying on being praised or rewarded for doing what others have decided they should do. If children are to feel competent in their learning and in all their activities, rather than adults being the judge, we need to encourage children to decide for themselves whether they were successful to their own standards. Of course children do value adults' praise, and we can help them to be strong learners by praising how well they showed the behaviour of good learners – concentrating, persevering, being enthusiastic and exploring, and the like.

Creating and thinking critically

This strand describes children's abilities to use their minds effectively

- to be original, creative thinkers
- to solve problems of all kinds
- to learn by connecting different ideas from their experiences
- to plan, develop and choose strategies for how to do things, changing approach as needed.

Creating and thinking critically – thinking

Having their own ideas

- **Thinking of ideas**
- **Finding ways to solve problems**
- **Finding new ways to do things**

Making links

- **Making links and noticing patterns in their experience**
- **Making predictions**
- **Testing their ideas**
- **Developing ideas of grouping, sequences, cause and effect**

Choosing ways to do things

- **Planning, making decisions about how to approach a task, solving a problem and reaching a goal**
- **Monitoring how effectively their activities are going**
- **Changing strategy as needed**
- **Reviewing how well the approach worked**

Having their own ideas

Creative thinking means coming up with new ideas in any situation and across all areas of learning, as well using imagination and artistic expression. It is supported when children have many open-ended opportunities to find their own ways to do things. Play is an ideal context for children to have and develop their own ideas. Adults can also support creative thinking by valuing and encouraging many possible solutions in open-ended discussions, and by ensuring that planned activities have scope for children to exercise their original thinking, rather than being done in just one way decided by the adult.

Making links

Children are making mental links in their experiences from birth, and making sense of everything they encounter. Initially this is an automatic process with the brain programmed to recognise patterns in experience, and this unconscious learning power continues throughout our lives. Gradually children become more aware of how they are thinking and of the connections they make, and are able to begin to control their own thinking processes.

Thinking is strongly supported by language. Putting thoughts into words – often through talking aloud to themselves – is an early stage in children thinking consciously about ideas. Adults help children by supporting them to talk about ideas, about what we think and about how we learn.

Choosing ways to do things

Intelligence is not something that is fixed for life, but can grow when we become more flexible in our thinking and can use our minds in a number of ways. Intelligence has been described as 'knowing what to do when you don't know what to do' – in other words, having at your disposal a number of possible ways to go about something.

Strategies are ways to do things which might be taught or developed independently. To function intelligently, instead of automatically doing things in a set way we need to
- think about our goal
- think about different possible approaches
- decide which strategy we will choose, or whether we need to create a new one
- put our plan into action
- keep an eye on whether it is working well
- carry on or change strategy if needed.

Adults can support children in each of these areas. We can be good models by talking about our own thinking and learning, and we can also support children to talk about these aspects of their activities. A 'plan-do-review' sequence helps children to be more conscious of the decisions they make, and to be stronger directors of their own learning.

15

Development Matters:
Supporting the Characteristics of Effective Learning – the adult role

	Positive Relationships: what adults could do	Enabling Environments: what adults could provide	What could be further developed in our practice?
Playing and Exploring (engagement) *Finding out and exploring* *Playing with what they know* *Being willing to 'have a go'*	• Play with children. Encourage them to explore, and show your own interest in discovering new things. • Help children as needed to do what they are trying to do, without taking over or directing. • Join in play sensitively, fitting in with children's ideas. • Model pretending an object is something else, and help develop roles and stories. • Encourage children to try new activities and to judge risks for themselves. Be sure to support children's confidence with words and body language. • Pay attention to how children engage in activities – the challenges faced, the effort, thought, learning and enjoyment. Talk more about the process than products. • Talk about how you and the children get better at things through effort and practice, and what we all can learn when things go wrong.	• Provide stimulating resources which are accessible and open-ended so they can be used, moved and combined in a variety of ways. • Make sure resources are relevant to children's interests. • Arrange flexible indoor and outdoor space and resources where children can explore, build, move and role play. • Help children concentrate by limiting noise, and making spaces visually calm and orderly. • Plan first-hand experiences and challenges appropriate to the development of the children. • Ensure children have uninterrupted time to play and explore.	
Active Learning (motivation) **Being involved and concentrating** **Keeping on trying** **Enjoying achieving what they set out to do**	• Support children to choose their activities – what they want to do and how they will do it. • Stimulate children's interest through shared attention, and calm over-stimulated children. • Help children to become aware of their own goals, make plans, and to review their own progress and successes. Describe what you see them trying to do, and encourage children to talk about their own processes and successes. • Be specific when you praise, especially noting effort such as how the child concentrates, tries different approaches, persists, solves problems, and has new ideas. • Encourage children to learn together and from each other. • Children develop their own motivations when you give reasons and talk about learning, rather than just directing.	• Children will become more deeply involved when you provide something that is new and unusual for them to explore, especially when it is linked to their interests. • Notice what arouses children's curiosity, looking for signs of deep involvement to identify learning that is intrinsically motivated. • Ensure children have time and freedom to become deeply involved in activities. • Children can maintain focus on things that interest them over a period of time. Help them to keep ideas in mind by talking over photographs of their previous activities. • Keep significant activities out instead of routinely tidying them away. • Make space and time for all children to contribute.	

Development Matters:
Supporting the Characteristics of Effective Learning – the adult role

	Positive Relationships: what adults could do	Enabling Environments: what adults could provide	What could be further developed in our practice?
Creating and Thinking Critically (thinking)	• Use the language of thinking and learning: think, know, remember, forget, idea, makes sense, plan, learn, find out, confused, figure out, trying to do. • Model being a thinker, showing that you don't always know, are curious and sometimes puzzled, and can think and find out.	• In planning activities, ask yourself: Is this an opportunity for children to find their own ways to represent and develop their own ideas? Avoid children just reproducing someone else's ideas. • Build in opportunities for children to play with materials before using them in planned tasks.	
Having their own ideas	• Encourage open-ended thinking by not settling on the first ideas: What else is possible? • Always respect children's efforts and ideas, so they feel safe to take a risk with a new idea.	• Play is a key opportunity for children to think creatively and flexibly, solve problems and link ideas. Establish the enabling conditions for rich play: space, time, flexible resources, choice, control, warm and supportive relationships.	
Making links	• Talking aloud helps children to think and control what they do. Model self-talk, describing your actions in play. • Give children time to talk and think.	• Recognisable and predictable routines help children to predict and make connections in their experiences. • Routines can be flexible, while still basically orderly.	
Choosing ways to do things	• Value questions, talk, and many possible responses, without rushing toward answers too quickly. • Support children's interests over time, reminding them of previous approaches and encouraging them to make connections between their experiences. • Model the creative process, showing your thinking about some of the many possible ways forward. • Sustained shared thinking helps children to explore ideas and make links. Follow children's lead in conversation, and think about things together. • Encourage children to describe problems they encounter, and to suggest ways to solve the problem. • Show and talk about strategies – how to do things – including problem-solving, thinking and learning. • Give feedback and help children to review their own progress and learning. Talk with children about what they are doing, how they plan to do it, what worked well and what they would change next time. • Model the plan-do-review process yourself.	• Plan linked experiences that follow the ideas children are really thinking about. • Use mind-maps to represent thinking together. • Develop a learning community which focuses on how and not just what we are learning.	

3

Areas of Learning and Development

There are seven areas of learning and development that must shape educational programmes in early years settings. All areas of learning and development are important and inter-connected.

Statutory Framework for the Early Years Foundation Stage 1.4

The characteristics of effective learning describe **how** babies and young children learn. The areas of learning and development describe **what** they learn through their playing and exploring, active learning and creating and thinking critically.

A key change in the revised EYFS is the shift from six areas of learning and development to seven.

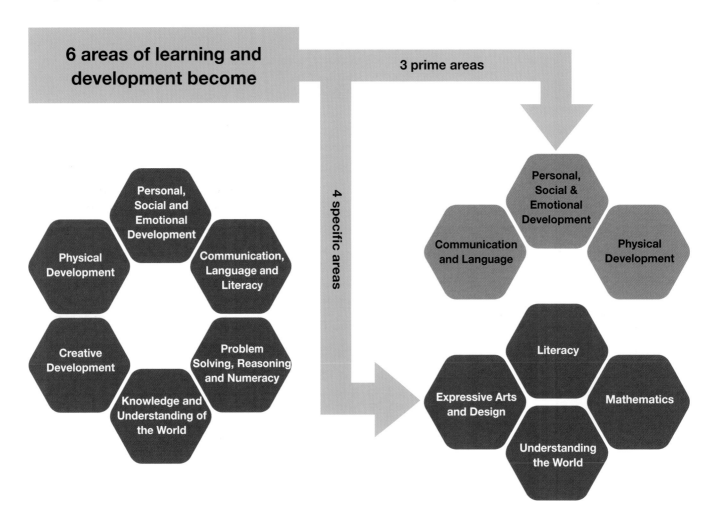

6 areas of learning and development become

3 prime areas

4 specific areas

Personal, Social and Emotional Development

Physical Development

Communication, Language and Literacy

Creative Development

Problem Solving, Reasoning and Numeracy

Knowledge and Understanding of the World

Personal, Social & Emotional Development

Communication and Language

Physical Development

Literacy

Expressive Arts and Design

Mathematics

Understanding the World

These seven areas consist of

three prime areas
- Personal, Social and Emotional Development
- Communication and Language
- Physical Development

four specific areas
- Literacy
- Mathematics
- Understanding the World
- Expressive Arts and Design

Why prime and specific?

- It is widely agreed by researchers, practitioners and parents that personal, social, and emotional development, communication and language and physical development are closely linked to one another and are central to all other areas of learning and development. (Angelou et al 2009 and Tickell review call for evidence 2010)

- Babies are 'primed' to encounter their environment through relating to and communicating with others, and engaging physically in their experiences. These three interdependent areas represent the earliest stages of development, which begin before birth and continue to occur within the early years when the developing brain has a maximum predisposition for learning.

- Other areas of learning are more specific to certain domains of knowledge and skill which are necessary for children's successful engagement in their particular society, and are identified as specific areas of learning and development.

- Children engage in activities which support their learning in specific areas by using their social, communicative and physical abilities, so that in the early years the prime areas are inseparable from all experiences.

Key differences between the prime and specific areas	
Prime	**Specific**
Time sensitive	**Less time sensitive**
If not securely in place between 3 and 5 years of age, they will be more difficult to acquire and their absence may hold the child back in other areas of learning.	Are less time-sensitive. Specific areas of learning reflect cultural knowledge and accumulated understanding. It is possible to acquire these bodies of knowledge at various stages through life.
Universal	**Culturally specific**
Occur in all communities and cultures.	Specific to priorities within communities and cultures.
Independent of the specific areas	**Dependent on the prime areas**
Not dependent on the specific areas of learning, although the specific areas of learning provide contexts for building on early development in the prime areas.	Are dependent on learning in the prime areas – the specific learning cannot easily take place without the prime.

The relationship between the prime and specific areas

- The specific areas provide a context for building on early development and learning beyond the prime areas.

- The specific areas are dependent on the prime areas and cannot be encountered in isolation from communication and language, personal, social and emotional development, and physical development, since the child is always experiencing the world through emotions, communication and physical and sensory involvement.

- Literacy, mathematics, understanding the world, and expressive arts and design are areas of learning that support young children's interest in the world around them and occur most commonly in adult-framed contexts. These specific areas of learning are influenced by the times we live in and society's beliefs about what is important for children to learn.

Why seven areas?

There are now seven areas because Communication, Language and Literacy has become two areas.

Communication, Language and Literacy

PRIME Communication and Language

SPECIFIC Literacy

The development of communication and language skills happens during an optimum window of brain development (and is therefore a prime area).

We can acquire literacy skills at any point in childhood or in adulthood. Becoming literate varies across cultures and relies on learning a body of knowledge including letter sound correspondence (and is therefore a specific area).

However this does not mean that literacy in its broadest sense should be left to later stages of the EYFS. Babies and very young children enjoy sharing books and mark-making begins at a very young age; these skills need to be fostered from infancy in a climate of talk about reading and writing as a child becomes increasingly aware of how communications are written down using words, letters and symbols.

Other changes to the Areas of Learning and Development

The names and aspects of each area of learning and development have been reviewed. Repetition across areas, and aspects which emphasised **how** children learn rather than **what** they learn (Characteristics of Early Learning) have been removed. The table below represents these changes.

EYFS 2008 Aspects of Areas of Learning and Development	Revised EYFS 2012 Aspects of Learning and Development
Personal Social and Emotional Development Making relationships Self-confidence and self-esteem Behaviour and self-control Dispositions and attitudes (now in *Characteristics*) Self-care (now in *Physical Development*) Sense of community (now in *Understanding the World*)	**Personal Social and Emotional Development (Prime Area)** Making relationships. Self-confidence and self-awareness Managing feelings and behaviour
Communication. Language and Literacy Language for thinking Language for communication	**Communication and Language** (Prime Area) Listening and attention Understanding Speaking
Reading Writing Linking sounds and letters Handwriting (now in *Physical Development*)	Literacy **(Specific Area)** Reading Writing
Physical Development Movement and space Using equipment and materials Health and bodily awareness	**Physical Development** (Prime Area) Moving and handling Health and self-care
Problem Solving, Reasoning and Numeracy Numbers as labels and for counting Calculating Shape, space and measures.	**Mathematics (Specific Area)** Numbers Shape, space and measures
Knowledge and Understanding of the World Communities Place Exploration and investigation (and also now in *Characteristics*) ICT Time (now in *Maths*) Designing and making (now in *Expressive Arts and Design*)	**Understanding the World (Specific Area)** People and communities The world Technology
Creative Development Exploring media and materials Creating music and dance Developing imagination and imaginative play Being creative (now in *Characteristics*)	**Expressive Arts and Design (Specific Area)** Exploring and using media and materials Being imaginative

Statutory Requirements covering the Areas of Learning and Development

The Statutory Framework briefly sets out the educational programmes and the early learning goals for each area. In addition some general guidance is provided in SF 1.7 to 1.9 on how all areas of learning and development should be delivered.

In these sections the importance of the prime areas is emphasised as well as the need to provide rich opportunities for all children to develop in their own unique ways although the 'school readiness' agenda is also present (see the introduction to this resource for more on this).

> *Practitioners must consider the individual needs, interests, and stage of development of each child in their care, and must use this information to plan a challenging and enjoyable experience for each child in all of the areas of learning and development.*
>
> *Practitioners working with the youngest children are expected to focus strongly on the three prime areas, which are the basis for successful learning in the other four specific areas. The three prime areas reflect the key skills and capacities all children need to develop and learn effectively, and become ready for school.*
>
> *It is expected that the balance will shift towards a more equal focus on all areas of learning as children grow in confidence and ability within the three prime areas. But throughout the early years, if a child's progress in any prime area gives cause for concern, practitioners must discuss this with the child's parents and/or carers and agree how to support the child.*
>
> *Practitioners must consider whether a child may have a special educational need or disability which requires specialist support. They should link with, and help families to access, relevant services from other agencies as appropriate.*
>
> *Statutory Framework for the Early Years Foundation Stage 1.7*

There is also an emphasis on the importance of play and interaction:

> *Each area of learning and development must be implemented through planned, purposeful play and through a mix of adult-led and child-initiated activity..............*
>
> *.......Practitioners must respond to each child's emerging needs and interests, guiding their development through warm, positive interaction.*
>
> *Statutory Framework for the Early Years Foundation Stage 1.9*

The description of implementing the areas of learning through 'planning purposeful play and through a combination of adult-led and child-initiated activity (SF 1.9) is explored in greater depth in the section on Organising Learning in this resource.

The importance of home language is also stressed for children learning English as an additional language.

> *For children whose home language is not English, providers must take reasonable steps to provide opportunities for children to develop and use their home language in play and learning, supporting their language development at home. Providers must also ensure that children have sufficient opportunities to learn and reach a good standard in English language during the EYFS, ensuring children are ready to benefit from the opportunities available to them when they begin Year 1.*
>
> *When assessing communication, language and literacy skills, practitioners must assess children's skills in English. If a child does not have a strong grasp of English language, practitioners must explore the child's skills in the home language with parents and/or carers, to establish whether there is cause for concern about language delay.*
>
> *Statutory Framework for the Early Years Foundation Stage 1.8*

Here 'school readiness' is confined to Year 1, although this might be interpreted as meaning that support in English will be unavailable after the end of the EYFS. As well as children who have a language delay or disorder and need further support through primary school, children can arrive in the country speaking little or no English at any age, and are entitled to support to access the curriculum.

There are also sections regarding the importance of key person relationship (SF1.11) and of a quality workforce (SF1.12). These areas are explored more fully in the sections on Key Person and Leading and Managing the EYFS in this resource.

Educational Programmes and Early Learning Goals

The rest of this section includes the educational programme and early learning goals for each area as they are set out in the Statutory Framework as well as briefly explaining the aspects of each area. The educational programmes, set out in the Statutory Framework 1.6, are extremely brief and provide only the headlines of what is involved in each area of learning.

The *Development Matters in the Early Years Foundation Stage* document provides detailed guidance on observing what children are learning plus examples of what practitioners might do and provide to support positive relationships and enabling environments across each aspect of each area. It also reminds practitioners that in every area children should be encouraged and supported to play and explore, be active in their learning, and to create and think critically. Page references for *Development Matters* (DM) are provided throughout the following section.

> *The Early Learning Goals are the expected outcomes at the end of the EYFS. In the 2008 Statutory Framework the Early Learning Goals were described as expectations for most children to reach by the end of the EYFS. ...by the end of the EYFS, some children will have exceeded the goals. Other children, depending on their individual needs, will be working towards some or all of the goals – particularly some younger children, some with learning difficulties or disabilities and some learning English as an additional language.*
>
> *Statutory Framework for the EYFS 2008 s2.6*

In the revised Statutory Framework this inclusive message with its recognition of diverse needs and abilities seems to have been diluted, merely saying:

> *The level of progress children should be expected to have attained by the end of the EYFS is defined by the early learning goals set out below.*
>
> *Statutory Framework for the Early Years Foundation Stage 1.13*

Statutory Framework section 2 on Assessment states that when compiling the EYFS Profile practitioners must indicate whether children are meeting these expected levels of development, exceeding them or not yet reaching them ('emerging'). Statutory Framework section 2.10 requires reasonable adjustments to be made for children with SEN and disabilities, but no mention is made of younger children or those learning EAL.

Referring to *Development Matters* will support practitioners to remember that the EYFS celebrates early childhood as stage in its own right, through which children pass in their own individual ways and at their own individual rates. Although many children will reach the early learning goals by the end of Reception, not all will. Each unique child needs to be valued for who they are as well as having plenty of time and space to learn. It is wrong to try and push children too far and too fast. Effective practitioners meet children where they are and walk with them in their learning, supporting and extending their experiences so they can make progress and do their very best – whether they meet the early learning goals or not.

The rest of this section includes the educational programme and early learning goal for each area as they are set out in the Statutory Framework (SF), as well as briefly explaining the aspects of each area and referring to further guidance in *Development Matters* (DM).

The Prime Areas

The Statutory Framework describes the prime areas as 'crucial for igniting children's curiosity and enthusiasm for learning, and for building their capacity to learn, form relationships and thrive'. These areas are listed throughout the statutory framework in the following order:
- Communication and Language
- Physical Development
- Personal, Social and Emotional Development

The ordering of these areas ignores recent research and the evidence from practitioners and parents presented to the Tickell review as well as the order advocated by the Tickell review report as to how children learn.

We would advocate that children are primed to encounter their environment through relating to and communicating with others, and engaging physically in their experiences. It is well known that, from birth, children's focus is drawn most strongly to other people, and learning and development occurs within the context of relationships. Communication and language development is not possible except in the context of responsive relationships - children cannot learn to communicate, use language, or build vocabulary, for instance, just from television; it must be in interaction with other people. In addition, there is increasing awareness of the underlying importance of early attachment and emotional well-being for successful cognitive and physical development and this should be given first priority.

In this resource we therefore listed the prime areas in the following order
- Personal, Social and Emotional Development
- Communication and Language
- Physical Development

Personal, Social and Emotional Development

Personal, social and emotional development involves helping children to develop a positive sense of themselves, and others; to form positive relationships and develop respect for others; to develop social skills and learn how to manage their feelings; to understand appropriate behaviour in groups; and to have confidence in their own abilities.

Statutory Framework for the Early Years Foundation Stage 1.6

There are three aspects of Personal, Social and Emotional Development
- Making relationships
- Self-confidence and self-awareness
- Managing feelings and behaviour

Making relationships is about social development – how we come to understand ourselves in relation to others, how we make friends, and behave towards others. The key person plays a key role in this process. See DM p9-10.

Self-confidence and self-awareness is about personal development – how we come to understand who we are and what we can do. Within the early years children begin to understand themselves as people, which supports developing confidence and motivation to engage pro-actively in the world. See DM p11-12.

Managing feelings and behaviour is about emotional development – how we come to understand our own and others' feelings and develop our ability to 'stand in someone else's shoes' and see things from their point of view, referred to as empathy, as well as how we come to understand the rules of society. See DM p13-15.

Early Learning Goals
By the end of the EYFS, normally at the end of the Reception year in school, it is expected that:

Making relationships	Self-confidence and self-awareness	Managing feelings and behaviour
Children play co-operatively, taking turns with others. They take account of one another's ideas about how to organise their activity. They show sensitivity to others' needs and feelings, and form positive relationships with adults and other children.	Children are confident to try new activities, and say why they like some activities more than others. They are confident to speak in a familiar group, will talk about their ideas, and will choose the resources they need for their chosen activities. They say when they do or don't need help.	Children talk about how they and others show feelings, talk about their own and others' behaviour, and its consequences, and know that some behaviour is unacceptable. They work as part of a group or class, and understand and follow the rules. They adjust their behaviour to different situations, and take changes of routine in their stride.

Communication and Language

*Communication and language involves giving
children opportunities to experience a rich language
environment; to develop their confidence and skills in
expressing themselves; and to speak and listen in a
range of situations*

*Statutory Framework for the Early Years Foundation
Stage 1.6*

There are three aspects of Communication
and Language
- Listening and Attention
- Understanding
- Speaking

These focus on the strands of language development
which are critical for later success and are drawn from
experience of implementing the Every Child a Talker
(ECAT) programme. Focusing on listening and attention
and separating receptive language (understanding) from
expressive language (speaking) promotes understanding
of how language develops, how best to support it and
how to identify children at risk of language delay.

Listening and attention Being able to focus attention
is a developmental ability underlying the acquisition
of language. Children's language development can
be enhanced by adults supporting children to focus
their attention effectively. Being able to attend is a
necessary skill supporting learning across all areas, and
is recognised as an aspect of cognitive self-regulation.
Listening and attention also underpins the ability to link
letters and sounds which supports reading and writing
development. See DM p16-17.

Understanding is supported by interaction with adults
who scaffold the development of vocabulary through
gesture and known words to help children interpret
spoken language. Understanding words and the meaning
of complex statements, questions, and linked sentences
is necessary in order to support reading, as well as
learning across all areas. See DM p18-19.

Speaking As children learn to communicate and talk,
they are empowered to participate fully with others – to
express their needs and feelings, their views and ideas.
This strand includes children learning to communicate in
a range of ways, including gesture and facial expressions.
The role of talk in shaping thought supports children to
solve problems, articulate reasoning, and talk about their
thinking and learning. Children need to acquire the ability to
express their feelings and thoughts in spoken language as
a precursor to using written language. See DM p20-22.

Early Learning Goals

By the end of the EYFS, normally at the end of the Reception year in school, it is expected that:

Listening and attention	Understanding	Speaking
Children listen attentively in a range of situations. They listen to stories, accurately anticipating key events and respond to what they hear with relevant comments, questions or actions. They give their attention to what others say and respond appropriately, while engaged in another activity.	Children follow instructions involving several ideas or actions. They answer 'how' and 'why' questions about their experiences and in response to stories or events.	Children express themselves effectively, showing awareness of listeners' needs. They use past, present and future forms accurately when talking about events that have happened or are to happen in the future. They develop their own narratives and explanations by connecting ideas or events.

Physical Development

*Physical development involves providing opportunities
for young children to be active and interactive; and to
develop their co-ordination, control, and movement.
Children must also be helped to understand the
importance of physical activity, and to make healthy
choices in relation to food.*

*Statutory Framework for the Early Years Foundation
Stage 1.6*

There are two aspects of Physical Development
• Moving and handling
• Health and self-care

Experience gained during physical activity promotes brain
development as well as strengthening muscles and the
cardiovascular system. Moving and manipulating also
contributes to learning because children first experience
concepts of the world through their bodies.

Moving and handling describes the importance of gross
and fine motor skills in children's physical development.
With each new physical ability – controlling eyes, limbs,
neck, being able to sit up unaided, becoming mobile – the
baby sees the world in a different way, and is able to test
and refine ideas from previous perceptions. Being able
to explore through movement enables a baby to make a
mental image or map of their surroundings, so they feel
secure and know where to find their familiar carer.

Large muscle control develops before fine motor skill,
and young children use large muscle activity to embody
ideas. Being able to manipulate materials is crucial
to developing understanding. For instance, young
children develop greater mathematical awareness of the
properties of shape and of number through handling
objects than through simply observing representations or
through formal instruction.

Exploring through large muscle activity, such as, tracing
shapes in the air, develops familiarity with writing
movements which will later become manageable in finer
movements for handwriting.

This aspect includes handwriting, since the tripod grip
and necessary wrist control are dependent on physical
development and are not part of the knowledge of
phoneme/grapheme correspondence necessary for
making meaning in writing English. As they reach the
end of the EYFS many children (especially boys) are
able to compose spellings to build words and construct
sentences but are not able to marshal all the physical
skills and hand-eye co-ordination necessary to write, so
their handwriting skills do not accurately represent their
compositional writing skills. See DM p23-25.

Health and self-care supports young children to be
healthy and stay safe. Children begin to understand more
about health and their own bodies through engaging in
physical play, having a balanced diet and learning about
healthy eating. When children have healthy experiences in
a setting where there are opportunities for energetic play,
for quiet contemplation and for bodily relaxation, they
develop understanding of how physical activities, food
and drink, sleep, safety and hygiene are vital to life.

As physical skills develop, children can engage in
activities that build their ability to act independently in
their environments – managing eating, toileting, and
dressing. Play in challenging but safe environments allows
children to take risks and helps develop awareness of
keeping themselves safe. See DM p27-28.

Early Learning Goals	
By the end of the EYFS, normally at the end of the Reception year in school, it is expected that:	
Moving and handling	**Health and self-care**
Children show good control and co-ordination in large and small movements. They move confidently in a range of ways, safely negotiating space. They handle equipment and tools effectively, including pencils for writing.	Children know the importance for good health of physical exercise, and a healthy diet, and talk about ways to keep healthy and safe. They manage their own basic hygiene and personal needs successfully, including dressing and going to the toilet independently.

The relationship between the prime areas

The prime areas of learning and development are closely connected to each other:

Personal, social and emotional development supports

- **physical development** as a child who feels secure and safe is confident to expand the boundaries of exploration and is motivated to reach, move and test physical capacities.
- **communication and language** within relationships which establish turn-taking, joint activity, a desire to communicate and understanding of shared meanings of words.

Communication and language supports

- **personal, social and emotional development** because a child who can communicate feelings, needs and ideas develops a strong sense of self, and is increasingly able to relate to others in rewarding and appropriate ways.
- **physical development** through description of actions which increase conscious control and through talk about health and the factors which influence this.

Physical development supports

- **personal, social and emotional development** as increasing physical control provides experiences of the self as an active agent in the environment, promoting growth in confidence and awareness of control.
- **communication and language** because a child who can effectively use large movements, gestures and the fine movements involved in speech is able to convey messages to others.

3
Areas of Learning and Development

The Specific Areas

Literacy

Literacy development involves encouraging children to link sounds and letters and to begin to read and write. Children must be given access to a wide range of reading materials (books, poems, and other written materials) to ignite their interest.

Statutory Framework for the Early Years Foundation Stage 1.6

There are two aspects of literacy
- Reading
- Writing

Reading is supported by all aspects of Communication and Language and is built on adults and children enjoying playing with, and acting out, rhymes and stories, as well as making books and engaging in role play activities. See DM p29-30.

Writing is supported by all aspects of Communication and Language and is built on children's developing knowledge of how written language works, gained through rhymes, books, stories and everyday examples of text around them. The roots of writing can be seen as children gradually begin to ascribe meaning to the marks they make, in order to record their communications for a wide range of purposes that have meaning for them. They begin to understand that language is composed of words and can hear the sounds in words. See DM p31-32.

Both Reading and Writing include the former 'Linking Sounds and Letters' as it is important that children do not grasp grapheme- phoneme correspondence in isolation, but have opportunities to apply their skills in meaningful ways. Thus the new aspects combine the acquisition of phonic knowledge and skills with their application to reading and writing essential for enjoyment and becoming a lifelong reader and writer.

Early Learning Goals
By the end of the EYFS, normally at the end of the Reception year in school, it is expected that:

Reading	Writing
Children read and understand simple sentences. They use phonic knowledge to decode regular words and read them aloud accurately. They also read some common irregular words. They demonstrate understanding when talking with others about what they have read.	Children use their phonic knowledge to write words in ways which match their spoken sounds. They also write some irregular common words. They write simple sentences which can be read by themselves and others. Some words are spelt correctly and others are phonetically plausible.

Mathematics

Mathematics involves providing children with opportunities to develop and improve their skills in counting, understanding and using numbers, calculating simple addition and subtraction problems; and to describe shapes, spaces, and measures.

Statutory Framework for the Early Years Foundation Stage 1.6

There are two aspects of Mathematics
- Numbers
- Shape, Space and Measures

Numbers includes the former aspect of calculating.

Evidence from EYFS Profile data in recent years illustrates that many children are able to recognise numbers and numerals but the same picture of attainment is not reflected in the application of this knowledge to solving problems by calculating. A significant factor in children's understanding of mathematics is the ability to talk about and apply their knowledge in ways that make sense to them and this is promoted in developing calculation as part of number knowledge. See DM p33-35.

Shape, Space and Measures includes some of the key mathematical skills that children will use throughout their lives, including telling the time. See DM p36-37.

Early Learning Goals
By the end of the EYFS, normally at the end of the Reception year in school, it is expected that:

Numbers	Shape, Space and Measures
Children count reliably with numbers from 1 to 20, place them in order and say which number is one more or one less than a given number. Using quantities and objects, they add and subtract two single-digit numbers and count on or back to find the answer. They solve problems, including doubling, halving and sharing.	Children use everyday language to talk about size, weight, capacity, position, distance, time and money to compare quantities and objects and to solve problems. They recognise, create and describe patterns. They explore characteristics of everyday objects and shapes and use mathematical language to describe them.

Understanding the World

Understanding the world involves guiding children to make sense of their physical world and their community through opportunities to explore, observe and find out about people, places, technology and the environment. Statutory Framework for the Early Years Foundation Stage 1.6

There are three aspects of Understanding the World
- People and communities
- The world
- Technology

People and communities acknowledges that children learn first about themselves and the people and things that are important to them. Children's learning is grounded in their own experiences, and their growing understanding of diversity and difference is informed by the reality of their own and other people's lives and of the different communities they encounter as they engage with the world. See DM p38-39.

The world focuses on the inter-relationship of people and communities and of living and non-living things. It supports children in experiencing the natural world and in understanding the difference between the natural and the made world. See DM p40-41.

Technology reflects the importance of children's growing understanding of simple mechanics as well as information and communication technology. See DM p42-43.

Early Learning Goals
By the end of the EYFS, normally at the end of the Reception year in school, it is expected that:

People and communities	The world	Technology
Children talk about past and present events in their own lives and in the lives of family members. They know that other children don't always enjoy the same things, and are sensitive to this. They know about similarities and differences between themselves and others, and among families, communities and traditions.	Children know about similarities and differences in relation to places, objects, materials and living things. They talk about the features of their own immediate environment and how environments might vary from one another. They make observations of animals and plants and explain why some things occur, and talk about changes.	Children recognise that a range of technology is used in places such as homes and schools. They select and use technology for particular purposes.

Expressive Arts and Design

Expressive arts and design involves enabling children to explore and play with a wide range of media and materials, as well as providing opportunities and encouragement for sharing their thoughts, ideas and feelings through a variety of activities in art, music, movement, dance, role-play, and design and technology.

Statutory Framework for the Early Years Foundation Stage (1.6)

There are two aspects of Expressive Arts and Design
- Exploring and using media and materials
- Being imaginative

Exploring and using media and materials focuses attention on children's experiences of exploring, learning about and building a repertoire of techniques for artistic expression and representation of their experiences across a range of media, including music and dance. See DM p44-45.

Being imaginative involves how children use what they have learnt in their own unique ways to represent ideas thoughts and feelings through a range of media.

Early Learning Goals
By the end of the EYFS, normally at the end of the Reception year in school, it is expected that:

Exploring and using media and materials	Being imaginative
Children sing songs, make music and dance, and experiment with ways of changing them. They safely use and explore a variety of materials, tools and techniques, experimenting with colour, design, texture, form and function.	Children use what they have learnt about media and materials in original ways, thinking about uses and purposes. They represent their own ideas, thoughts and feelings through design and technology, art, music, dance, role-play and stories.

29

4

Organising for learning

Each area of learning and development must be implemented through planned, purposeful play and through a combination of adult-led and child-initiated activity.

Play is essential for children's development, building their confidence as they learn to explore, to think about problems, and relate to others.

Children learn by leading their own play, and by taking part in play which is guided by adults.

There is an ongoing judgement to be made by practitioners about the balance between activities led by children, and activities led or guided by adults.

Practitioners must respond to each child's emerging needs and interests, guiding their development through warm, positive interaction.

As children grow older, and as their development allows, it is expected that the balance will gradually shift towards more activities led by adults, to help children prepare for more formal learning, ready for Year 1.

Statutory Framework for the Foundation Stage 1.9

It is understandably difficult to define in a brief legal framework how play and learning are connected for young children, and how early years settings should plan and implement activities. Researchers and educators continue to discuss and study this in detail, reflecting on the nature of play in early years settings, how best to plan for play and learning, and the role of the adult. Responses to the consultation on the draft EYFS framework showed that fewer than 4 in 10 people thought the proposed description was clear, and the slight amendments which appear in the final version are unlikely to have resolved the uncertainties.

Questions and issues for practitioners and settings to consider in relation to their own practice

What is 'planned, purposeful play'?

- Play might be defined as an open-ended activity, freely chosen by and under the control of the player.
- Play is open to spontaneous ideas as they arise, so any initial plans about what to play, how to play and who to play with can change from moment to moment.
- In play the player finds their own purpose – it might be enjoyment, challenge, social interaction, exploring things or ideas, practising and perfecting skills.

How can adults provide for 'planned purposeful play'?

- While adults cannot plan or choose the purposes in children's play, they can plan *for* play.
- Adults plan for children's rich, purposeful play when they
  - plan and provide the indoor and outdoor environment, resources, and time for children to become engrossed in their play.
  - plan to ensure that there are opportunities to play in many different ways, with experiences related to all areas of learning and development.
  - supplement resources and arrange the environment in flexible ways to respond to children's agendas in terms of their interests and ways of playing, and to stimulate children's play and explorations.

Why is there a combination of child-initiated and adult-led activities?

- Play is a key context for children's learning – not only across the areas of learning but also in developing learning power as described in the Characteristics of Effective Learning. Ensuring children can initiate their own activities provides opportunities for play.
- There are many other ways children learn, as well. They learn through taking part in real life activities, such as cooking, gardening, or shopping. They learn through having conversations, listening to stories, being shown how to do things, imitating what they see others do, being told about things.
- Adults have a responsibility to pass on to children important knowledge and skills, including things which they might miss out on if they don't happen to encounter certain experiences in their chosen play. Adult-led activity can ensure that children have opportunities to develop in all important areas of learning.

What is 'play which is guided by adults'?

- When adults plan and lead activities, this is not really play – and children do not consider it to be play. The activities, however, can be fun and **playful** and provide good learning opportunities.
- **Playful adult-led activities** will ensure there is active participation by the children, and that they are able to make choices and use their own ideas within the activity.
- Adults also **join in with children's play**, and can bring an extra dimension to the learning that arises in play. They may
  - develop children's communication and language through having a conversation, talking in role play or providing vocabulary to describe events
  - encourage children to solve the problems that emerge in play
  - model and support building a story together in role play
  - support a child to participate with others
  - support children to focus their attention
  - discuss ideas and strategies
  - suggest a new direction or challenge.

An effective adult observes and thinks carefully about whether and when to join in play. Children's play without adults sometimes can be dull and repetitive, and may benefit from stimulation from the adult. On the other hand, play without adults can bring the strongest opportunities for children to be independent learners – and there is a risk that the play may be interrupted or highjacked by adult intervention. Adults need to consider why they might join in and whether they will bring something positive to support or extend the learning. The adult tries to be a sensitive support and follow the child's lead, avoiding taking over the direction of the play or limiting the children's own control and thinking.

How do practitioners make a judgement about the balance of child-initiated and adult-led activities?

There are many factors that play a part in establishing a mix in individual settings, for example:

- **the age and developmental stage of the children**
  Babies and toddlers can be introduced to adult-planned activities, but cannot be expected to participate if they are not actively attracted and captivated by what is on offer. Older children gradually become able to consciously direct their attention and participate for brief periods in adult-led small group activities.
- **the pattern of attendance for individual children**
  A child who attends for a full day may need some open-ended, unstructured time while other children in the setting only for a short session are focussing on a planned activity. A child spending a few hours with a childminder after a school day similarly would benefit from relaxed time in open-ended self-chosen activity.

A predictable routine helps children to feel confident and in control of their circumstances, so it is useful to establish an overall structure to times for child-initiated and adult-led activity. This can be adjusted to suit different groups of children, and can be flexible within the overall pattern in order to accommodate children's needs.

Within both play and in adult-led activities, there is a more subtle shifting of who is taking the lead at any given moment.
The adult can be the 'guide at the side', while the child is an active learner in both contexts.

- In play the adult may temporarily take the lead by showing the child how to do something, posing a question or challenge, or making a suggestion.
- In playful adult-led activities the child can pose questions and make suggestions, and take the activity in original and unexpected directions.

Rather than trying to come up with a precise formula for the best balance of activities, it is useful to think of all the possibilities as a continuum that runs from completely unstructured to highly structured activities.

Unstructured	Child-initiated play	Focused learning	Highly structured
Play without adult support	Adult support for an enabling environment, and sensitive interaction	Adult-guided, playful experiential activities	Adult-directed, little or no play

The shaded area shows the kind of activity that best supports children's learning. The key message here is that they are different dimensions of the same thing – that children and adults together are partners in learning. The shift along the continuum from one to another can be fluid and adaptable to different children's needs and circumstances.

Diagram from Learning, Playing and Interacting: Good Practice in the EYFS, DCSF 2009, 00775-2009BKT-EN

What happens to play for children nearing the end of the EYFS?

- The Statutory Framework suggests that 'the balance will gradually shift toward more activities led by adults, to help children prepare for more formal learning, ready for Year 1.'
- A gradual shift which is appropriate to children's development can be seen within the bigger context of a gradual shift across the age range, from how practitioners work with babies and young toddlers – where most of the activity is child-initiated – to working with children in the reception year, as shown in the diagram below.

Unstructured	Child-initiated play	Focused learning	Highly structured
Play without adult support	Adult support for an enabling environment, and sensitive interaction	Adult-guided, playful experiential activities	Adult-directed, little or no play

Youngest children   Older children

- Good educational provision at all stages should be geared to the approaches that best help children to learn, and many would argue that 'formal learning' – centred in the 'highly structured' end of the continuum above – is not the most effective approach for children in Year 1 of the primary curriculum.

- Children are supported to be 'ready' for their future experiences by being supported to be confident and resilient, which comes through rich and appropriate early childhood experiences.

- Making demands on a child now because it may be expected later, risks infringing on what children need to build the strong foundation which supports their future learning and development. We do not require tiny babies to practise holding their own weight and impose leg exercises because one day they will be expected to walk. Instead we provide the right opportunities for babies to gradually develop the abilities and strengths that will later enable them to walk.

- Five-year-olds will benefit from and be able to participate in fairly brief adult-led group activities, particularly in small groups, and they can learn effectively in very brief highly structured activities planned for specific purposes. This does not mean that play has lost its value, and it should not be squeezed out of their experience.

All children, throughout the EYFS, have a right to the balance of play, child-initiated and adult-led activities, indoors and outdoors, which meets their **current** needs and helps them to be strong and active learners.

5

Key Person

All the commitments of the EYFS expect practitioners to 'tune in' to children as unique individuals. This involves:

- knowing about how children develop
- observing children closely
- listening actively, attentively, and with respect, to all children and parents whatever their background
- valuing what you learn from observing children and from talking with their parents and acting on it for the benefit of the children
- understanding that physical and mental health and well-being are closely related

These commitments are for everyone – whether a leader and manager having oversight and responsibility for all the children, or a practitioner working with a smaller group or class.

In addition there is a legal requirement that every setting implement a key person system so that every child and family has a 'special' relationship with one member of staff. There is a new emphasis on the key person's role in working with parents in order to support learning and development in the home – see the Partnership with Parents section in this resource.

> **Each child must be assigned a key person (a safeguarding and welfare requirement - see paragraph 3.26). [In childminding settings the childminder is the key person.] Providers must inform parents and/or carers of the name of the key person, and explain their role, when a child starts attending a setting. The key person must help ensure that every child's learning and care is tailored to meet their individual needs. The key person must seek to engage and support parents and/or carers in guiding their child's development at home. They should also help families engage with more specialist support if appropriate.**
>
> **Statutory Framework for the Early Years Foundation Stage 1.11**

> **Each child must be assigned a key person. Their role is to help ensure that every child's care is tailored to meet their individual needs (in accordance with paragraph 1.11), to help the child become familiar with the setting, offer a settled relationship for the child and build a relationship with their parents.**
>
> **Statutory Framework for the Early Years Foundation Stage 3.26**

The key person role is vitally important for all children in the EYFS because it is within positive relationships and interactions that we all learn to be confident, self-assured, happy people who can understand others, make friends and open our minds and bodies to exploring and learning about the world.

The key person supplements important relationships and learning that start from birth. Babies are vulnerable and totally dependent on others for survival. When they learn that they can depend on and trust one person (usually, but not always, their mother) who is consistently responsive and sensitive to their physical and emotional needs they have what is called a 'secure attachment'. However, no one person can provide everything a growing child needs and children can form close attachments with several people.

A child with secure attachment feels able to rely on their special adults or key people for safety and comfort, and uses these important attachment relationships as bases from which to explore and learn about the world. These emotional relationships underpin the characteristics of effective learning (see section 2 of this resource.)

The EYFS commitment to key person explains the role

> *A key person has special responsibilities for working with a small number of children, giving them reassurance to feel safe and cared for and building relationships with their parents.*
>
> **EYFS card 2.4**

This requirement applies to all children in the EYFS.

> *Even when children are older and can hold special
> people in mind for longer there is still a need for
> them to have a key person to depend on in the
> setting such as their teacher or a teaching assistant.*
>
> **EYFS card 2.4**

Sometimes a 'key person' is understood to be a named
person to manage record-keeping for the child. Whilst an
administrative system is important, it is not the same as a
key-person system. A key-person system is not primarily
about administrative tasks and record-keeping, but is
about positive relationships.

The difference between approaching working with
children as a set of tasks and seeing it as building
relationships based on knowledge of and respect for
particular children is well illustrated by Julian Grenier:

> *Taking this approach means that a child experiences
> an adult who is 'tuned in', who can develop a
> special and personal relationship with the child.
> In an impersonal nursery anyone and everyone
> changes nappies at a time that is convenient to
> the organisation. Children may be processed
> across the nappy- changing table like tins of beans
> travelling along the checkout [at a supermarket].
> The key person changes nappies in the context of
> a relationship with the child. If just anyone changes
> nappies, wipes noses and rocks children to sleep,
> then there are no special relationships. The care of
> the children becomes just another task alongside
> mopping floors and cleaning tables.*
>
> **Extract from J.Grenier, All About... Developing Positive
> Relations with Children, Nursery World, Volume 105,
> Issue 3971, 2nd June 2005.**

As adults we can all feel stressed and insecure. Think, for
example, about what it feels like to arrive at a party where
you don't know anyone else, or to be starting work in a
new environment. It is so reassuring when someone smiles
and says hello and introduces you to others; or when
you meet the person who will be your mentor and they
explain the workplace systems and routines. It is good to
have someone we can rely on until we feel confident to
manage the situation on our own. Even then, knowing they
are there, and will support us if necessary, often gives us
confidence to do things we might otherwise avoid. This is
what key people do for their allocated group of children.
The key person relationship is fundamental to each child's
well-being, learning and development.

Parents tune in to their children by:

- Being engaged (providing one-to-one time)
- Being accessible (possibly occupied with others or engaged in tasks, but available)
- Being emotionally available (able to empathise and talk about feelings)
- Taking responsibility (for everyday care and welfare)

In the key person approach, particular adults (not many or all adults) provide those dimensions in their relationships with key children.

The EYFS card as well as *Development Matters* explore many of the ways that practitioners can be effective key persons. Here are just a few examples:

Being engaged

- Hold and handle babies, since sensitive touch helps to build security and attachment.
- Plan one to one time to talk with and listen to your key children's parents.
- Plan one to one time to talk with and listen to your key children and give your full attention when children look to you for a response.
- Find out through talking with parents and observation about things at home and in the setting which are important to the child: their favourite toys, songs, rhymes and games they like to play.
- Develop a shared understanding with parents (and other adults important to the child) of the child's responses and how these are different at home and in the setting, for example, how they show that
  - they are happy, sad, angry, excited;
  - they are hungry, thirsty, tired, hot, cold;
  - they want a cuddle or need some time alone.
- Be aware of focusing support through 'doing' as well as 'saying'. Sitting at the baby or child's level, smiling and nodding as they explore, offers the wordless reassurance that all children will seek. For some young babies, children with special educational needs and those learning English as an additional language this will often be more supportive than talk, which may sometimes be too challenging.

Being accessible

- Sitting at the snack table, for example, rather than standing tidying a wall cupboard, shows new key children that you although you may be talking to others and engaged in an activity they can easily find you. Your reaction when they do – reaching out to them, smiling, including them in conversation with other children- will all help build the key person relationship.
- The key person also needs to be accessible to parents. Plan time to share and reflect with parents on children's progress and development, ensuring appropriate support is available where parents do not speak or understand English.
- Nobody can be there all the time, so ensure that each key person is paired with a 'buddy' who knows the family as well, and can step in when necessary.

Being emotionally available

- Understand the need to reassure some parents that the role of the key person is to supplement, not replicate or undermine, the love and attention that parents give their child.
- At times of transition (such as shift changes) make sure staff greet and say goodbye to babies and their carers. This helps to develop secure and trusting three-way relationships. Even when children are older - in reception class, for example – be sensitive to their need for consistency and the stressful feelings that may be involved in coping with changes of staff and environment at playtime and lunchtimes.
- Demonstrate active listening and model awareness of the feelings of others. For instance acknowledge the child's feelings when a child is upset. 'I can see you're feeling sad. Shall we go and get a tissue, and then you can tell me what has made you so sad,' rather than 'Come on, it was only a slight bump and he didn't mean it - cheer up'.
- Encourage children to listen to each other and notice each other's feelings. If another child is hurt or upset for instance talk about how that child is feeling. Help other children to console them by stroking their arm or cuddling them.
- Introduce into conversation simple words for feelings and mental states like 'happy', 'sad', 'cross', 'hurt' and 'scared'. This helps children start to learn about words that express feelings and about what they are feeling themselves. You might say, for example, 'You like playing in the sandpit, don't you? It makes you happy.'

Taking responsibility

- Discuss the cultural needs and expectations for skin and hair care with parents prior to entry to the setting, ensuring that the needs of all children are met appropriately and that parents' wishes are respected.
- Change nappies in the context of a relationship with the child, making it a time to talk and be close.
- Support children's growing independence as they do things for themselves, such as pulling up their pants after toileting, recognising different parental expectations.
- Plan support for children who have not yet made friends.
- Ensure all children have time to relate to their key person, individually and in small groups.

Supporting the key person

Being a key person is a very demanding role. All key people will need support and help with some of the challenges and dilemmas, for example **how to maintain sufficient professional distance whilst still being emotionally engaged with the children and parents.**

Sometimes, practitioners may feel overwhelmed by the crying of children (and sometimes parents) who are experiencing separation. Or they may respond angrily when a child hurts another. In these situations it is helpful to be able to step back and talk with colleagues about what is going on for the children. This often helps us gain a sense of perspective and recognise that our professional duty is to control our own emotions and respond calmly to these situations. Where the child is hurting others we may then understand more about their anger and frustration and what their apparent unkindness may tell us about their emotional state. This helps us think about how the adults can provide support, and set appropriate limits if necessary. As with all good early years practice, the best way to address this and other dilemmas is through observation and discussion, and using professional judgement

Staff teams need to think about how they look after and promote personal, social and emotional well-being for everybody in the setting, not just the children. It is well documented that unless the needs of the adults working with young children are considered, so that they feel respected, valued and looked after, they are unlikely to be able to do their best to utilise their skills and knowledge to promote the health and welfare of the young children in their care.

In a setting where practitioners have high levels of self-awareness and empathy they are able to 'tune in' and respond in a reflective rather than an impulsive way. The relationships they establish with the children and the learning opportunities they provide will help children to develop the personal, social and emotional skills they need as well as feelings of belonging and emotional well-being.

As Grenier et al so accurately observe:

This is an emotionally demanding and skilful area of practice that some practitioners find overwhelming and so avoid becoming close to children. Yet those that are able to be available, sensitive and responsive to their key children can take pride in knowing that not only are they contributing positively to the quality of their key child's mental model of relationships for the future, they are also assisting healthy brain development and learning abilities. Research indicates that an effective key-person approach leads to:

- more satisfied and engaged staff;
- improved care and learning for children;
- parents who feel confident about the quality and devotion of professional staff.

From *Social and Emotional Aspects of Development: guidance for practitioners working in the EYFS (DCSF 2008).* Appendix 3, The key person in Reception classes and small nursery settings, by Julian Grenier, Peter Elfer, Julia Manning Morton, Katie Dearnley and Dilys Wilson.

6

Partnership working

Partnership with Parents

About 70% of children's lives are spent not in a setting, but with their family and the wider community. Home and community must be recognised as significant learning environments in the lives of children, and research shows that the activities that take place at home have the largest impact on children's learning. Successful relationships between parents and educators can have long-lasting and beneficial effects on children's learning and well-being. Relationships become **partnerships** when there is two-way communication and parents and practitioners really listen to each other.

The introduction to the EYFS Statutory Framework (SF III) affirms that the EYFS seeks to provide 'partnership working between practitioners and with parents and/or carers', and in section 1 asserts the need for providers to work 'in partnership with parents to promote the learning and development of all children' (SF1.1) There are further references to working with parents throughout the Statutory Framework.

The key person (see section 5 of this resource) must seek to 'engage and support parents and/or carers in guiding their child's development at home' (SF 1.11) and 'offer a settled relationship for the child and build a relationship with their parents' (SF 3.26).

In Section 1 of the Statutory Framework there are references to certain concerns that must be discussed with parents and Section 3.60 stresses the need to provide a space for private conversation.

- If a child's progress in any prime area gives cause for concern, practitioners must discuss this with the child's parents and/or carers and agree how to support the child. (SF 1.7).
- If a child does not have a strong grasp of English language, practitioners must explore the child's skills in the home language with parents and/or carers, to establish whether there is cause for concern about language delay. (SF 1.8).

There are several references to parents in Section 2 of the Statutory Framework (Assessment), where the need for partnership is again stressed, as well as the need

to share observations. References to parents appear throughout Section 3 (The Safeguarding and Welfare Requirements) particularly in relation to information and records (SF 3.67 to 3.75). For example

> **Providers must make the following information available to parents and/or carers:**
>
> - how the EYFS is being delivered in the setting, and how parents and/or carers can access more information (for example, via the DfE website);
> - the range and type of activities and experiences provided for children, the daily routines of the setting, and how parents and carers can share learning at home;
> - how the setting supports children with special educational needs and disabilities;
> - food and drinks provided for children;
> - details of the provider's policies and procedures (all providers except childminders must make copies available on request) including the procedure to be followed in the event of a parent and/or carer failing to collect a child at the appointed time, or in the event of a child going missing at, or away from, the setting; and
> - staffing in the setting; the name of their child's key person and their role; and a telephone number for parents and/or carers to contact in an emergency.
>
> **Statutory Framework for the Early Years Foundation Stage 3.72**

In summary, the Statutory Framework is quite specific about some aspects of working with parents, but it is up to providers to develop the sort of relationships with parents that will enable the 'strong partnership' of the Enabling Environment' principle and the Commitment to 'Parents as Partners' (card 2.2) to flourish in practice.

- Parents and practitioners share a joint interest in, and responsibility for, children's development and learning. Both parents and practitioners are key people in building children's self-esteem and dispositions to learn, although they bring different perspectives and expertise. Parents are experts on their own child and practitioners are experts on all children's learning and development.

Children usually feel more confident and positive about themselves and their learning when parents and practitioners work together in an atmosphere of mutual respect, and value each other's views and support in achieving the best outcomes for each child.

The first step in building relationships is **respectful communication**. All settings communicate with parents in a range of ways, sometimes without realising it. Posters, pictures and other resources will communicate the setting's attitudes to disability and to ethnic, cultural and social diversity. However, no amount of welcoming displays in community languages or positive images of disabled people will compensate for a lack of friendliness and warmth from staff. You do not have to be bilingual, or indeed know any words of another person's language, to make them feel welcome.

Parents will feel valued by the setting if
- Resources and displays represent the ethnic, cultural and social diversity in society.
- They can see their own family background and culture represented as well as those of others.
- They always get a warm and genuine greeting.
- They do not see other parents being treated better than they are.
- Staff pronounce parents' and children's names correctly.
- Staff are flexible and able to cope with the unexpected twists and turns of family life.

When settings **ask parents what they need from practitioners**, their comments usually include the following. Someone who
- really likes my child and knows them well;
- listens, and doesn't just tell us what to do;
- understands if we are a bit late arriving;
- cares about me as well as my child;
- gives me time to talk;
- smiles and has a sense of humour;
- helps my child learn;
- keeps me informed.

When practitioners are friendly professionals with a genuine interest in the children, parents come to like and trust them, and mutual respect can flourish.

- Being a parent is rewarding but often demanding. Some parents have not had good role models from their own parents and being able to work with practitioners who model consistent loving relationships with young children is very supportive for them and their children.

- Practitioners can offer advice and assistance to ease parents and children through emotionally-charged times such as weaning, toilet training or tantrums. Knowing that what your child is doing is a normal part of a young child's development can be very reassuring. If there is cause for further concern, practitioners can offer advice and coping strategies.

Becoming co-researchers in children's learning
Research is about asking questions and finding out more. In this context it is small scale and focused on a shared interest in individual children and how adults can support and extend their learning.

- Parents draw on their own experiences of education when they formulate their expectations of early childhood settings and the skills of practitioners who work in them.
- Effective settings can help them become co-researchers of their child's learning and development by sharing their knowledge and supporting their learning as well as their children's. One way to do this is to take a family learning approach where parents work in a group together with a practitioner on an area such as early literacy. They explore current thinking about how children become literate from birth onwards, they discuss how the setting supports children's communication and language development and what they themselves do, or could do, at home. They carry out activities with their children both in the setting and at home and come back again the next week to share their findings.

There are endless possibilities which will depend on the context of the setting. Parents and children may work together with an artist or on creating an outdoor area, they may think about how emotional well-being is developed through play, and document their child's experience at home to share with practitioners. Whatever the activity, it is something that practitioners and parents share and where they acknowledge their different but complementary expertise.

Parents who are informed about the ways in which children learn, think about and represent their thoughts through talk, drawing and action are in a better position to support the continuity and progression of their children's learning and development between home and early years setting. Practitioners who are informed about how children learn and behave at home and in the wider community can better support their learning in the setting.

What about parents who are unable or unwilling to work alongside practitioners?

- Not all parents will have time to attend sessions in a setting but many will respond positively to being asked to record their child's play or favourite things at home, possibly with a loaned or disposable camera.

- Many parents are happy to be kept informed and enthused about what is happening in the setting via email, text or twitter and are more likely to respond when any response can be short and instant.

- Practitioners often talk about 'hard to reach' parents but it is often the setting that is 'hard to reach' for the parents. It is important to think about how accessible you are – not just in terms of the setting's physical position in the community but how welcoming you are to those who are less confident. Do you know who is not using your services and can you find ways of going to them, rather than expecting them to come to you?

One of the greatest benefits to early years practitioners in working with parents is the encouragement it gives to making the setting's approaches to learning and teaching more open and shared. When this happens it is easier for parents to get involved in the drafting of policies and procedures and to feel really valued as their child's first and most enduring educators.

Partnership with other Professionals

There are only four references in the Statutory Framework to working with other professionals, and none at all to 'multi-agency' or 'multi-professional' work. However these requirements, albeit briefly, ensure that where appropriate, providers are responsible for making relationships with other professionals that support children and families.

Practitioners should address any learning and development needs in partnership with parents and/ or carers, and any relevant professionals.

Statutory Framework for the Early Years Foundation Stage 2.2

If there are significant emerging concerns, or an identified special educational need or disability, practitioners should develop a targeted plan to support the child's future learning and development involving other professionals (for example, the provider's Special Educational Needs Co-ordinator) as appropriate.

Statutory Framework for the Early Years Foundation Stage 2.3

Practitioners should encourage parents and/or carers to share information from the progress check with other relevant professionals...................Providers must have the consent of parents and/or carers to share information directly with other relevant professionals, if they consider this would be helpful.

Statutory Framework for the Early Years Foundation Stage 2.5

Providers must maintain records and obtain and share information (with parents and carers, other professionals working with the child, and the police, social services and Ofsted as appropriate).

Statutory Framework for the Early Years Foundation Stage 3.67

The EYFS commitment to The Wider Context (card 3.4) reminds us

Working in partnership with other settings, other professionals and with individuals and groups in the community supports children's development and progress towards the outcomes of Every Child Matters : being healthy; staying safe; enjoying and achieving; making a positive contribution and economic well-being.

Card 3.4 also reminds us about the importance of working together with other providers in the interests of continuity for children making transitions

Transitions and continuity

- Children may move between several different settings in the course of a day, a week, a month or a year.

- Children's social, emotional and educational needs are central to any transition between one setting and another or within one setting.

- Some children and their parents will find transition times stressful while other will enjoy the experience.

- Effective communication between the settings is key to ensuring that children's needs are met and there is continuity in their learning.

- Working together across services may involve working with other local settings as well as home visitors such as Home Start and Portage workers, health or social care professionals, SEN and other inclusion services and librarians. To best support children and their families all these groups need to communicate well, listen carefully to all concerned and to put the children's needs first. Together we can have a far deeper understanding of the children we work with and therefore provide higher quality learning experiences for children.

- The professional background of workers can be both a strength and a barrier to multi-agency working. As each profession has developed its own language and body of knowledge, it not only serves to provide a professional identity but can alienate those outside the profession who do not share their language or way of thinking.
- Professionals may also be used to working differently. For example, health professionals and social workers tend to work with individuals or small groups on identified needs. Their work tends to be with targeted groups of people who have particular needs. Settings, on the other hand, work with large groups of children and provide a universal service.

Some ideas for effective practice:
- Have a policy on transition and continuity which involves parents and is shared with everyone involved within and beyond the setting.
- When children attend several settings ensure that practitioners from each setting regularly share observations and involve parents in this process.
- Take time to listen to colleagues from other professional backgrounds and be open about differences of language and approach.

Partnership with the Community

EYFS Card 3.4 underlines the value of seeing the child in the context of the community as well as the family and setting.

The community
- Every setting is part of its community even though not all the children may live in the surrounding neighbourhood.

- The local community may contain many different racial, cultural or religious groups. Even if it doesn't, there will be children and adults of various ages with different views, beliefs and backgrounds using the setting.

- When the setting values the local community it can encourage the different community groups to work together for the benefit of all.

The EYFS seeks to provide 'Equality of opportunity and anti-discriminatory practice, ensuring that every child is included and supported' (SF III). The introduction to *Development Matters* reminds us that:

Children have a right, spelled out in the United Nations Convention on the Rights of the Child, to provision which enables them to develop their personalities, talents and abilities irrespective of ethnicity, culture or religion, home language, family background, learning difficulties, disabilities or gender.

Seeing the setting as part of the community will help to promote good relationships and understanding of difference and diversity. There are examples throughout *Development Matters* of what practitioners could do and provide. Here are a few:
- Ensure that each child is recognised as a valuable contributor to the group.
- Celebrate and value cultural, religious and community events and experiences.
- Provide positive images of all children including those with diverse physical characteristics, including disabilities.
- Encourage children to talk about their own home and community life, and to find out about other children's experiences.
- Help children to learn positive attitudes and challenge negative attitudes and stereotypes, e.g. using puppets, Persona Dolls, stories and books showing black heroes or disabled kings or queens or families with same sex parents, having a visit from a male midwife or female fire fighter.
- Visit different parts of the local community, including areas where some children may be very knowledgeable, e.g. Chinese supermarket, local church, elders lunch club, Greek café.

7 Assessment

The Statutory Framework calls for two levels of assessment in the EYFS. It describes ongoing **formative assessment** in general terms, and then specifies requirements for **summative assessment** at two points – age two, and the end of the EYFS.

Formative Assessment

Practitioners must consider the individual needs, interests, and stage of development of each child in their care, and must use this information to plan a challenging and enjoyable experience for each child in all of the areas of learning and development.

Statutory Framework for the Early Years Foundation Stage (1.7)

Assessment plays an important part in helping parents, carers and practitioners to recognise children's progress, understand their needs, and to plan activities and support. Ongoing assessment (also known as formative assessment) is an integral part of the learning and development process. It involves practitioners observing children to understand their level of achievement, interests and learning styles, and to then shape learning experiences for each child reflecting those observations. In their interactions with children, practitioners should respond to their own day-to-day observations about children's progress, and observations that parents and carers share.

Statutory Framework for the Early Years Foundation Stage (2.1)

Formative assessment is rightly given high priority at the centre of early years practice. In order to support every unique child, we must first discover who that child is. Only then can we ensure that we respond by doing our best to match the child's needs.

We discover the uniqueness of each child through skilful **observation**.

The formative assessment cycle begins with **noticing what the child does and says**. It is important to observe closely how the child responds to experiences with people, things and events. The individuality of the child comes through when we watch with real fascination, and a desire to really know the child. This requires an awareness of and sensitivity to the many ways that children communicate.

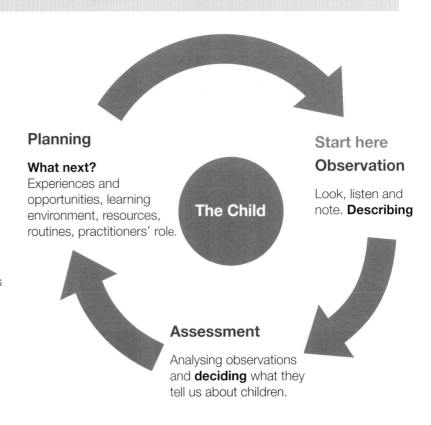

Planning

What next?
Experiences and opportunities, learning environment, resources, routines, practitioners' role.

The Child

Start here
Observation

Look, listen and note. **Describing**

Assessment

Analysing observations and **deciding** what they tell us about children.

In the **assessment** part of the cycle we then consider what we have observed the child to do or say, putting the clues together to understand more about who the child is. Possibly it tells us something about the child's

- feelings – pleasures, fears, excitements, security, and so on
- preferences
- interests and current preoccupations in what they are learning
- ways of approaching the world around them
- ways of thinking and learning
- skills and knowledge.

Deciding what we think the observation might tell us about a child is our assessment. An assessment is not a fact, unlike the observation which should describe what actually happened. The assessment is a judgement – an interpretation of what has been observed. In order to make an assessment, a practitioner draws on many aspects of their professional knowledge and skill, including knowledge of child development and knowledge of how learning develops across different areas. A good assessment also depends on using emotional intelligence, as well as awareness of the context, the culture, family and home experiences. What parents and carers share about the child outside of the setting provides crucial information to help practitioners and parents together to understand and interpret what they observe.

Assessment, then, can never be drawn from just one observation, but needs to be grounded in a more rounded awareness of the whole child. **Formative assessment is ongoing** because

- getting to know a child builds gradually, across many contexts and over time
- new observations may link to what was observed earlier, and help practitioners to understand the bigger picture in a new light
- children's interests and the focus of their current learning shift and turn in unpredictable ways, and skilful practitioners remain alert to meet and support the child at the edge of their current learning.

Planning involves deciding how best to respond to the child to support their learning, based on our understanding of the child. We might plan to respond in order to support the child's

- well-being
- interests
- ways of learning
- competence and confidence with current skills and knowledge
- progress in skills and knowledge.

There are a number of 'tools' available to the practitioner to support learning. Planning may include

- ways of interacting with the child – such as being alongside, conversations and discussions, questions, suggestions, modelling, demonstrating
- enhancing available resources within the continuous provision
- rearranging the spaces in the physical environment outside or inside
- adjusting how time is organised within daily routines
- providing specific activities.

Settings will have their own approaches to planning on a **short-term** basis. Some arrange regular planning discussions, perhaps weekly or every two weeks, where team members can share their observations and reflections, and consider what to plan in response. Short term plans might respond to

- one particular child's needs, interests, and learning, with the plan geared to the individual child
- observations and reflections on one child, with the plan offered to all the children to use the learning opportunity in their own ways
- observations and reflections on a group of children, which might prompt plans relevant to that specific group, or alterations to the provision that will offer different opportunities to all the children.

Practitioners use formative assessment in a much more on-going way, however, than simply at periodic short term planning meetings. **Moment-to-moment** planning describes the way that practitioners go around the observe-assess-plan cycle within all their interactions with children on a continuous basis, hundreds of times each day. Practitioners tune into individual children's signals and communications (observation), consider what this means (assessment), and decide how to respond in the next moment (planning). **This is where the real potential for supporting children's learning lies, since it allows adults accurately and immediately to meet and support a child according to individual needs and circumstances. It is within this sensitive, skilful and responsive interaction that practitioners can best be a learning partner for each unique child.**

Being able to provide this quality of responsive interaction, also known as contingency, requires considerable awareness and respect for each child's personality and individual learning pathway, backed up by knowledge of child development and learning theories. The non-statutory guidance *Development Matters in the Early Years Foundation Stage* (Early Education 2012) gives an overview of typical development and supports practitioners to reflect on individual children's own pattern of development across the areas of learning and development. It also provides examples to prompt reflection on how practitioners can respond to support children along their own pathway, through interactions within positive relationships and through enhancing the enabling environment. **Download *Development Matters* from www.foundationyears.org.uk or www.early-education.org.uk**

Paperwork

Assessment should not entail prolonged breaks from interaction with children, nor require excessive paperwork. Paperwork should be limited to that which is absolutely necessary to promote children's successful learning and development.

Statutory Framework for the Early Years Foundation Stage (2.2)

This section of the Statutory Framework might be usefully posted on the wall of every early years setting, and shared with any visitors who seem to be pressing for vast amounts of detailed evidence to prove that the setting is observing, assessing and using that information to plan appropriately stimulating, challenging and enjoyable experiences for children. Reducing paperwork which is a burden on practitioners and takes them away from their core job – being a responsive partner alongside children – was a key aim of the EYFS revision, and the resulting message deserves large notice:

Paper work should be limited to that which is absolutely necessary to promote children's successful learning and development.

Perhaps inspectors will reflect this statement by asking not 'Where is the paper trail to prove your responsive planning?' but instead asking 'Why was it necessary to record this much information? Are you sure it did not take practitioners away from their work with the children?' Settings can review their own systems to determine whether there is unnecessary paperwork at the moment, and refine their way of working to reach the minimum which supports effective practice. There is no single description of how much paperwork is enough, because different settings and practitioners work in different circumstances and will make their own decisions about how much of their thinking process needs to be recorded. The following points may help in considering the right level:

- Collecting evidence for inspection or other purposes which are not essential to children's learning and development comes second to the work of supporting children.
- Evidence can be verbal as well as written – be ready to give examples, based on what is happening in your setting on any given day, which demonstrate that you have responded (planned) based on what you observed children to do and say.
- Written plans can be very brief and sketchy, with a note of a child or children's initials to indicate the observational spark for the planned activity or enhancement to the environment.
- Paperwork is also an issue in relation to summative assessment (see below). Your evidence for making summative judgements is what you have observed – what children do and say. But these observations do not necessarily need to be recorded – you hold a lot of information in your mind, and can give verbal examples alongside a minimum of written records.

Why record on-going assessments? To find the right amount of recording, consider your reasons. How might your written records or photographs help to support children's learning and development? For example:
- Recorded observations can **highlight significant moments of learning** to share with
  - parents
  - children so they can reflect on their own learning
  - other members of staff.
- Write down only the 'wow moments' instead of wasting time on routine matters
- Written records can **supplement the practitioner's memory**. This may be more important where a setting has larger numbers of children to get to know. In any busy setting, however, it is useful to make a quick note of significant observations which might otherwise be forgotten.

- Records help when **reflecting back on a child's progress over time**, and sometimes help to prompt ideas about the links in a child's learning
- Where there is any **particular concern about a child**, written observations can be a useful support in careful assessment, planning, and review of the effectiveness of provision to meet the child's individual needs. In such cases there would be more observational evidence than for children where there is no particular concern.

Summative Assessment

As well as assessing and planning for children's learning on an on-going basis, another level of assessment involves periodically standing back to get an overview of the progress a child is making in their learning and development.

Summative assessment involves comparing a child's level of attainment with a description of what would be typical for children of roughly the same age. It must be based on all the detailed knowledge of the child gained through formative assessment over time, and should include the insights and perspective of others who know the child in other contexts – particularly the parents/carers who know the child best, as well as other relevant professionals in and beyond the setting – and should reflect as far as possible the point of view of the child.

Summative assessment can help to
- Ensure that practitioners have a **clear understanding of a child's progress** across important areas of learning and development
- Share with parents in considering a child's progress and **how best to support their learning and development in the setting and at home**
- **Identify any concerns** in order to plan prompt support to meet children's needs
- Consider the **quality of the provision** in supporting children to make progress, and identify where there may be areas for improvement in the setting.

Leaders and managers can compile the information from summative assessment of all the children to look closely at the progress of the group as a whole, individual children, and particular groups such as boys/girls or children learning English as an additional language. Asking questions about what the data shows may point out improvements that could be made in the setting to ensure that children are being given the best opportunities to learn, and that staff have the skills and knowledge they need to help all children progress.

Further information for leaders and managers to use summative assessment to improve the quality of their provision is available in *Progress Matters: Reviewing and enhancing young children's development (DCSF 2009)*.

There are potential pitfalls to avoid in the summative assessment of young children's progress. It is important to bear in mind that children all develop in different ways and at different rates, and there should be no expectation of exact norms to compare children against. On the other hand, there is a general pattern of typical development across the early years and parents and practitioners want to know when a child is progressing well, as well as where there may be very quick progress or a risk of delay.

Best-fit judgement

A check-list approach to assessing progress assumes that all children will and should demonstrate exactly the same order and rate of development, and specifies individual elements of what they can do.

A best-fit approach acknowledges that there will be many individual variations within an overall typical pattern.

Why not a checklist? When practitioners assess progress by using a list of separate statements of what children can do, highlighting or ticking them off individually, this is a check-list approach. It risks reducing practitioners' understanding of the complexity of children's individual learning journeys and leading to expectations that children's pathways will follow a predictable route, each identical to the other, and each prescribed in advance. Research shows that children's learning is not linear, progressing smoothly from one step to the next, but occurs in overlapping waves, with stops and starts, reverses, plateaus and spurts.

The outline of development across EYFS age/stage bands shown in the *Development Matters* guidance makes it very clear that this should not be used in this way. Every page carries this reminder:

'Children develop at their own rates, and in their own ways. The development statements and their order should not be taken as necessary steps for individual children. They should not be used as checklists. The age/stage bands overlap because these are not fixed age boundaries but suggest a typical range of development.'

Best-fit judgements, on the other hand, make it possible to consider the overall progress a child is making, and whether progress is generally in line with what is typical for a child of that age. The child's learning and development is compared with a band of descriptors, such as the *Development Matters* bands, to see whether it roughly gives a picture of the child, and the band is identified which most closely describes the child.

There are two particular elements to making a best-fit judgement which help to acknowledge that individual differences are to be expected

- **The child is not assumed to precisely match the descriptors** – There is no expectation that every element of the descriptors must be evidenced individually, and it is also understood that the child is likely to show many aspects that are not listed in the descriptors.
- **The child is not expected to reach milestones at a specified age** – The age/stage bands in *Development Matters* overlap, and so the child's age is considered within a wider view of the typical variations in rate of development.

With these two points in mind, it is possible to

- **decide on the age/stage band which most closely describes the child's development.**
- **identify whether the child is broadly on track for their age, ahead of the typical level of development, or making slower progress than is typical.**
- **provide a brief statement that shows the individuality of the child within the areas of learning and development, as well as interests and ways of learning.**

Progress information for all the children in the setting can be compiled into data which leaders and managers can use to analyse how well they are helping children to progress, including looking at groups such as boys and girls or those learning English as an additional language in order to consider particular needs.

Identifying possible concerns

Practitioners are often anxious about describing a child's development as lagging behind what might be expected. Parents also express concerns about whether their child could wrongly be labelled as having a difficulty. At the same time, parents say they do want an accurate picture of the progress a child is making.

Where a child is seen to be making slower progress, it is important to bear in mind that the assessment is not labelling or diagnosing a problem. It is simply identifying where the child's development is in relation to most children. It is important to be positive about children's achievements, but it can be unhelpful to focus only on what the child can do and the progress being made, without pointing out gaps and slower areas. That approach assumes that progress will occur in the child's own time, and risks missing vital opportunities to provide the best experiences to support children's learning and development.

It is true that children may well move forward more quickly with no special attention, and may be following their own developmental pace and pattern – and that awareness should be part of a positive approach to any discussion about a child's summative assessment. At the same time, a positive approach also includes considering whether the best opportunities and support for the child are in place, deciding how to maximise support at home and in the setting, and agreeing to keep a watchful eye on the child's progress. Enhancing the learning environment and interactions may well help the child to progress more quickly. If not, parents and practitioners can then consider seeking extra advice and support.

Progress check at age two

> When a child is aged between two and three, practitioners must review their progress, and provide parents and/or carers with a short written summary of their child's development in the prime areas. This progress check must identify the child's strengths, and any areas where the child's progress is less than expected.
>
> **Statutory Framework for the Early Years Foundation Stage (2.3)**

The summative progress check between the ages of two and three is a new requirement of the revised EYFS, aimed particularly at promoting early intervention to meet the needs of vulnerable children and families. There is growing awareness of the importance of the earliest years in brain development, and the long-term impact of early opportunities to develop socially, emotionally, and in language ability. Support for children and improvements in the home learning environment within the first three years have been shown to have a much greater effect than waiting to address concerns when children are in school.

The Statutory Framework lists the following **requirements**:

- Agree with parents and/or carers when is the most useful time for the summary
- Provide parents and or/carers with a short written summary of children's development in the prime areas
- Identify strengths and any areas where progress is slower than expected, including areas where additional support might be needed
- Describe activities and strategies in the setting to address issues or concerns
- Discuss with parents and/or carers how learning can be supported at home
- If it is considered helpful to share the information directly with other professionals, first obtain parent/carer's permission.

In addition, the Statutory Framework says that practitioners **should**:

- Decide what else to include in the summary beyond the targeted areas – for example, it may be helpful to describe how the child learns in terms of the characteristics of effective learning.

- Develop a targeted plan with other professionals if there are significant concerns or an identified special educational need or disability, for example through the setting Special Educational Needs Coordinator
- Complete the progress check if a child moving between settings has spent most time in their setting
- Encourage parents to share information with other professionals, including their health visitor to inform the Healthy Child Programme review at age two, and with other settings.

There is no prescribed format for the written summary at age two. Many settings already have a summative system in place which can easily be used or adapted for this purpose.

Further guidance and examples of written summaries are available in ***A Know How Guide: The EYFS progress check at age two*** (NCB and DfE 2012). **Download from http://www.foundationyears.org.uk**. This guide provides a useful set of principles and approaches to the progress check. It is particularly helpful in outlining effective partnership with parents, ensuring that the summary is not a one-way communication but is developed together by practitioners and parents.

EYFS Profile – assessment at the end of the EYFS

> In the final term of the year in which the child reaches age five, and no later than 30 June in that term, the EYFS Profile must be completed for each child. The Profile provides parents and carers, practitioners and teachers with a well-rounded picture of a child's knowledge, understanding and abilities, their progress against expected levels, and their readiness for Year 1.
>
> **Statutory Framework for the Early Years Foundation Stage (2.6)**

What stays the same? The requirement for a summative assessment at the end of the EYFS has been in place for some years. Normally completed by the reception teacher in June, the EYFS Profile is based on formative assessment and contributions from parents and other professionals. It is shared with parents, and with Year 1 teachers to inform them about the children's learning and development and enable them to plan effectively.

Unlike the progress check at two, the results are reported to the local authority, which has a duty to pass them on to the government. Moderation activities are carried out by local authorities, supporting greater reliability of the data through helping teachers to make consistent and accurate judgements.

What has changed?

> Each child's level of development must be assessed against the early learning goals. Practitioners must indicate whether children are meeting expected levels of development, or if they are exceeding expected levels, or not yet reaching expected levels ('emerging'). This is the EYFS Profile.
>
> **Statutory Framework for the Early Years Foundation Stage (2.7)**

The revised EYFS Profile is now aligned exactly with assessment against the early learning goals, with **one judgement to be made for each of the 17 early learning goals** – unlike the previous Profile where there were 117 possible separate scale points, alongside 69 early learning goals.

The EYFS Profile has been greatly streamlined, but it does not cover a reduced view of children's learning and development. It still includes all the areas of learning and development in order to give a holistic picture. The separate judgements to be made have been reduced because the early learning goal (ELG) is used to describe a band of attainment, and a **best-fit judgement** records whether the child is described by each ELG, or is still working towards or exceeding the ELG.

Guidance and exemplification of completing the EYFS Profile will be issued by the Standards and Testing Agency in the autumn of 2012, and will be available to **download from www.foundationyears.org.uk**.

> Year 1 teachers must be given a copy of the Profile report together with a short commentary on each child's skills and abilities in relation to the three key characteristics of effective learning. These should inform a dialogue between Reception and Year 1 teachers about each child's stage of development and learning needs and assist with the planning of activities in Year 1.
>
> **Statutory Framework for the Early Years Foundation Stage (2.8)**

There is a new requirement for the Profile to contain information on **how** the child learns, and not just what they have achieved. This will take the form a brief statement about the child in terms of the three characteristics of effective learning, which will be shared with Year 1 teachers in discussion about the children and supporting both what they learn and the children as learners.

8

Safeguarding and Welfare

To emphasise the importance of safeguarding the welfare requirements are now called the Safeguarding and Welfare Requirements. They make up half of the Statutory Framework (Section 3). Some of them have already in been mentioned in the context of other sections. These requirements are the basics which must be in place to keep children safe and comply with the law. There are not many changes to those set out in the original framework although safeguarding and child protection have been highlighted. **The DfE has provided a guide entitled 'Overall reforms to the 2012 EYFS framework' that can be downloaded from www.foundationyears.org.uk**

1. **Child protection:** the revised EYFS includes examples of adults' behaviour which might be signs of abuse and neglect. If they become aware of any such signs, staff should respond appropriately in order to safeguard children.

2. The EYFS now requires that safeguarding policies and procedures must cover the use of mobile phones and cameras in the setting.

3. **Suitable people:** the requirements for providers to check the suitability of managers have been simplified. From September 2012, providers will be responsible for obtaining criminal record disclosures on managers. Currently, Ofsted obtain these disclosures.

4. **Staff qualifications, training, support and skills:** a requirement has been introduced in relation to staff supervision. Providers must give staff opportunities for coaching and training, mutual support, teamwork, continuous improvement, and confidential discussion of sensitive issues.

5. The requirement for childminders to complete training in the EYFS has been strengthened. Childminders will be required to complete the training before they register with Ofsted.

6. **Staff to child ratios:** there is a clarification of the circumstances in which there may be exceptions to the staff to child ratios for childminders caring for children of mixed ages.

7. **Safety and suitability of premises, environment and equipment:** the requirements in relation to risk assessment have been adjusted to clarify that it is for providers to judge whether a risk assessment needs to be recorded in writing.

Leading and Managing the EYFS

Although there is very little explicit reference to management in the Statutory Framework, and none to leadership, clearly the EYFS needs both leadership and management for the requirements to be met for the benefit of children and families. Indeed the statutory framework is written primarily for people in charge of schools and settings, as it is their ultimate responsibility to ensure that legal requirements are met.

What is meant by leadership and management?
These are terms which are used together and often interchangeably, and much has been written on both. Most writers see them as complementary with leadership viewed as the vision and influence to inspire and initiate change, and management being more about everyday organisation.

- In the context of the Statutory Framework leaders and managers are understood to be the named person in overall charge of the setting and school
- However children and their parents look to all early years practitioners for leadership and management as they go about the daily business of organising their group or class, making decisions and 'being in charge'. The people who will be the 'Head of Centre', 'Headteacher', or 'Nursery Manager' in the future are learning some of the skills they need to lead and manage a larger group of adults and children in their current roles
- Childminders may not think of themselves as leaders and managers when working in their own homes, but they too are the person in charge, to whom children and parents turn. If they are working with colleagues or are network co-ordinators their role also involves leading and managing adults.

Leadership and management at any level are about learning and development. Settings, and the adults working in them, grow and develop in response to positive relationships and enabling environments – just like the children. It is the responsibility of leaders and managers to provide an ethos where this growth, development and continuous improvement can take place. The Statutory Framework is clear that the quality of provision for children depends on the quality of the workforce.

A quality learning experience for children requires a quality workforce. A well qualified, skilled staff strongly increases the potential of any individual setting to deliver the best possible outcomes for children. Requirements in relation to staff qualifications are outlined in Section 3. Providers should regularly consider the training and development needs of all staff members to ensure they offer a quality learning experience for children that continually improves.

Statutory Framework for the Early Years Foundation Stage 1.12

The early years workforce has never been better qualified but there is still a long way to go, and the requirements are the bare minimum.

In group settings, the manager must hold at least a full and relevant level 3 qualification and at least half of all other staff must hold at least a full and relevant level 2 qualification. The manager should have at least two years' experience of working in an early years setting, or have at least two years' other suitable experience. The provider must ensure there is a named deputy who, in their judgement, is capable and qualified to take charge in the manager's absence.

Statutory Framework for the Early Years Foundation Stage 3.21

All maintained nursery and primary schools and many settings in the private, voluntary and independent sector have managers and staff who are far better qualified than these minimum requirements. But the fact that level 2 is still acceptable for half the staff and level 3 plus two years 'suitable' experience for the person in charge, results in the early years sector still having a long way to go in terms of universal quality provision for young children.

In times of economic hardship and decreased funding for early years it may be difficult for providers or individual practitioners to finance the acquisition of further qualifications and this is recognised in SF 3.22 where language like 'wherever possible' and 'should consider' is used.

Providers should ensure that regular staff appraisals are carried out to identify any training needs, and secure opportunities for continued professional development for staff. Providers should support their staff to improve their qualification levels wherever possible. For staff without a relevant qualification, providers should consider supporting them to obtain a relevant level 2 qualification.

Statutory Framework for the Early Years Foundation Stage 3.22

So in reality it may not be through further formal qualifications that providers comply with the Statutory Framework and 'ensure they offer a quality learning experience for children that continually improves'. It may be through recognising the importance of the requirement for regular supervision for continuous improvement.

Supervision

Providers must put appropriate arrangements in place for the supervision of staff who have contact with children and families. Effective supervision provides support, coaching and training for the practitioner and promotes the interests of children. Supervision should foster a culture of mutual support, teamwork and continuous improvement which encourages the confidential discussion of sensitive issues.

Statutory Framework for the Early Years Foundation Stage 3.19

Supervision should provide opportunities for staff to:
- *discuss any issues – particularly concerning children's development or well-being;*
- *identify solutions to address issues as they arise; and*
- *receive coaching to improve their personal effectiveness.*

Statutory Framework for the Early Years Foundation Stage 3.20

Supervision is a term that school practitioners may not be as familiar with as those who have experience working in or with social care or health. The key elements are the **support, coaching and training and the focus on children, as well as personal development**. School performance management arrangements may differ in language, and possibly emphasis, but also have the aim of continuous improvement. It is up to head teachers to ensure that the early years staff have the opportunities outlined in the supervision requirements.

The key which underpins all effective leadership and management is the 'culture of mutual support, teamwork and continuous improvement'. Everything that this resource has so far discussed about working with children has been based on respecting and valuing children as powerful learners with unique personalities and attributes, who deserve to be valued for who they are, regardless of culture and background. A setting which truly values children and families will be very likely also to value its staff.

- Being kind, considerate and listening to others is the basis of a valuing and emotionally intelligent culture. It is unfair, for example, to expect young children to develop empathy if practitioners talk about children, parents or members of staff in unkind terms as soon as their backs are turned. Children may not always understand the words adults use, but they have very good radar for tone and feeling.
- Valuing leads to trusting and is based on staff experiencing a sense of their own value within an organisation and feeling comfortable about their own abilities and needs. Through supportive relationships within the organisation they reflect upon practice in dialogue with colleagues, and work together to create change and improvement in the setting, confident of support.

This diagram below represents how this cycle of professional development works in settings, not only to value all who learn and work there, but also to create a learning community for children, staff and parents. The basis is an approach which sees practitioners, parents and children as co-researchers in children's learning. The ethos and values are those held by each individual, as well as discussed and developed together as a setting. They are informed by the principles and commitments of the EYFS as well as experience, knowledge and understanding of children's entitlements for learning and development.

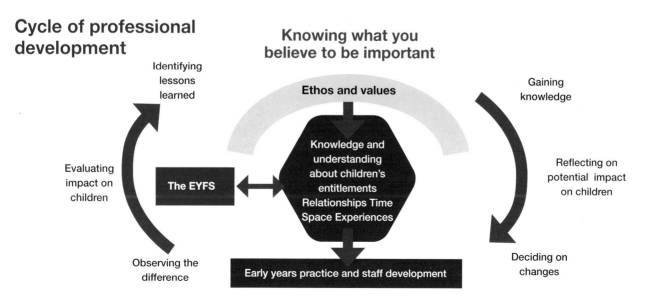

Cycle of professional development

Knowing what you believe to be important

Identifying lessons learned

Ethos and values

Gaining knowledge

Evaluating impact on children

The EYFS

Knowledge and understanding about children's entitlements Relationships Time Space Experiences

Reflecting on potential impact on children

Observing the difference

Early years practice and staff development

Deciding on changes

Making changes

10

Appendix

Statutory Framework for the Early Years Foundation Stage (2012)

Setting the standards for learning, development and care for children from birth to five

This framework is mandatory for all early years providers (from 1 September 2012)[1]: maintained schools, non-maintained schools, independent schools, and all providers on the Early Years Register[2]. The learning and development requirements are given legal force by an Order made under Section 39(1)(a) of the Childcare Act 2006. The safeguarding and welfare requirements are given legal force by Regulations made under Section 39(1)(b) of the Childcare Act 2006.

Ofsted has regard to the Early Years Foundation Stage (EYFS) in carrying out inspections, and reports on the quality and standards of provision. Ofsted publishes inspection reports at www.ofsted.gov.uk. Ofsted may issue a notice to improve (in respect of any failure to meet a requirement in the document), and/or may issue a welfare requirements notice (in respect of Section 3). It is an offence for a provider to fail to comply with a welfare requirements notice.

Introduction

I. Every child deserves the best possible start in life and the support that enables them to fulfil their potential. Children develop quickly in the early years and a child's experiences between birth and age five have a major impact on their future life chances. A secure, safe and happy childhood is important in its own right. Good parenting and high quality early learning together provide the foundation children need to make the most of their abilities and talents as they grow up.

II. The Early Years Foundation Stage (EYFS) sets the standards that all early years providers must meet to ensure that children learn and develop well and are kept healthy and safe. It promotes teaching and learning to ensure children's 'school readiness' and gives children the broad range of knowledge and skills that provide the right foundation for good future progress through school and life.

III. The EYFS seeks to provide:

- **quality and consistency** in all early years settings, so that every child makes good progress and no child gets left behind;

- **a secure foundation** through learning and development opportunities which are planned around the needs and interests of each individual child and are assessed and reviewed regularly;

- **partnership working** between practitioners and with parents and/or carers;

- **equality of opportunity** and anti-discriminatory practice, ensuring that every child is included and supported.

IV. The EYFS specifies requirements for learning and development and for safeguarding children and promoting their welfare. The **learning and development requirements** cover:

- *the areas of learning and development which must shape activities and experiences (educational programmes)* for children in all early years settings;

- *the early learning goals* that providers must help children work towards (the knowledge, skills and understanding children should have at the end of the academic year in which they turn five); and

- *assessment arrangements* for measuring progress (and requirements for reporting to parents and/or carers).

V. The safeguarding and welfare requirements cover the steps that providers must take to keep children safe and promote their welfare.

---

[1] Section 46 of the Childcare Act 2006 enables the Secretary of State to confer exemptions from the learning and development requirements in certain prescribed circumstances.

[2] The Childcare (Exemptions from Registration) Order 2008 (S.I.2008/979) specifies the circumstances in which providers are not required to register.

Overarching principles

VI. Four guiding principles should shape practice in early years settings. These are:

- every child is a **unique child**, who is constantly learning and can be resilient, capable, confident and self-assured;

- children learn to be strong and independent through **positive relationships**;

- children learn and develop well in **enabling environments**, in which their experiences respond to their individual needs and there is a strong partnership between practitioners and parents and/or carers; and

- **children develop and learn in different ways and at different rates**. The framework covers the education and care of all children in early years provision, including children with special educational needs and disabilities.

Section 1 – The Learning And Development Requirements

1.1 This section defines what providers must do, working in partnership with parents and/or carers, to promote the learning and development of all children in their care, and to ensure they are ready for school. The learning and development requirements are informed by the best available evidence on how children learn and reflect the broad range of skills, knowledge and attitudes children need as foundations for good future progress. Early years providers must guide the development of children's capabilities with a view to ensuring that children in their care complete the EYFS ready to benefit fully from the opportunities ahead of them.

1.2 The EYFS learning and development requirements comprise:
- the seven areas of learning and development and the educational programmes (described below); the early learning goals, which summarise the knowledge, skills and understanding that all young children should have gained by the end of the Reception year; and

- the assessment requirements (when and how practitioners must assess children's achievements, and when and how they should discuss children's progress with parents and/or carers).

Wrap around and holiday providers

1.3 Wrap around[3] and holiday providers[4] should be guided by, but do not necessarily need to meet, all the learning and development requirements. Practitioners should discuss with parents and/or carers (and other practitioners and providers as appropriate) the support they intend to offer, seeking to complement learning in settings in which children spend more time.

The areas of learning and development

1.4 There are seven areas of learning and development that must shape educational programmes in early years settings. All areas of learning and development are important and inter-connected. Three areas are particularly crucial for igniting children's curiosity and enthusiasm for learning, and for building their capacity to learn, form relationships and thrive. These three areas, the prime areas, are:
- communication and language;
- physical development; and
- personal, social and emotional development.

1.5 Providers must also support children in four specific areas, through which the three prime areas are strengthened and applied. The specific areas are:
- literacy;
- mathematics;
- understanding the world; and
- expressive arts and design.

1.6 Educational programmes must involve activities and experiences for children, as follows.
- **Communication and language** development involves giving children opportunities to experience a rich language environment; to develop their confidence and skills in expressing themselves; and to speak and listen in a range of situations.
- **Physical development** involves providing opportunities for young children to be active and interactive; and to develop their co-ordination, control, and movement. Children must also be helped to understand the importance of physical activity, and to make healthy choices in relation to food.

[3] Care offered before and after a school day, e.g. by an after school club or by a childminder.

[4] Provision exclusively in the school holidays.

- **Personal, social and emotional development** involves helping children to develop a positive sense of themselves, and others; to form positive relationships and develop respect for others; to develop social skills and learn how to manage their feelings; to understand appropriate behaviour in groups; and to have confidence in their own abilities.
- **Literacy** development involves encouraging children to link sounds and letters and to begin to read and write. Children must be given access to a wide range of reading materials (books, poems, and other written materials) to ignite their interest.
- **Mathematics** involves providing children with opportunities to develop and improve their skills in counting, understanding and using numbers, calculating simple addition and subtraction problems; and to describe shapes, spaces, and measures.
- **Understanding the world** involves guiding children to make sense of their physical world and their community through opportunities to explore, observe and find out about people, places, technology and the environment.
- **Expressive arts and design** involves enabling children to explore and play with a wide range of media and materials, as well as providing opportunities and encouragement for sharing their thoughts, ideas and feelings through a variety of activities in art, music, movement, dance, role-play, and design and technology.

1.7 Practitioners must consider the individual needs, interests, and stage of development of each child in their care, and must use this information to plan a challenging and enjoyable experience for each child in all of the areas of learning and development. Practitioners working with the youngest children are expected to focus strongly on the three prime areas, which are the basis for successful learning in the other four specific areas. The three prime areas reflect the key skills and capacities all children need to develop and learn effectively, and become ready for school. It is expected that the balance will shift towards a more equal focus on all areas of learning as children grow in confidence and ability within the three prime areas. But throughout the early years, if a child's progress in any prime area gives cause for concern, practitioners must discuss this with the child's parents and/or carers and agree how to support the child. Practitioners must consider whether a child may have a special educational need or disability which requires specialist support. They should link with, and help families to access, relevant services from other agencies as appropriate.

1.8 For children whose home language is not English, providers must take reasonable steps to provide opportunities for children to develop and use their home language in play and learning, supporting their language development at home. Providers must also ensure that children have sufficient opportunities to learn and reach a good standard in English language during the EYFS, ensuring children are ready to benefit from the opportunities available to them when they begin Year 1. When assessing communication, language and literacy skills, practitioners must assess children's skills in English. If a child does not have a strong grasp of English language, practitioners must explore the child's skills in the home language with parents and/or carers, to establish whether there is cause for concern about language delay.

1.9 Each area of learning and development must be implemented through planned, purposeful play and through a mix of adult-led and child-initiated activity. Play is essential for children's development, building their confidence as they learn to explore, to think about problems, and relate to others. Children learn by leading their own play, and by taking part in play which is guided by adults. There is an ongoing judgement to be made by practitioners about the balance between activities led by children, and activities led or guided by adults. Practitioners must respond to each child's emerging needs and interests, guiding their development through warm, positive interaction. As children grow older, and as their development allows, it is expected that the balance will gradually shift towards more activities led by adults, to help children prepare for more formal learning, ready for Year 1.

1.10 In planning and guiding children's activities, practitioners must reflect on the different ways that children learn and reflect these in their practice. Three characteristics of effective teaching and learning are:
- **playing and exploring** - children investigate and experience things, and 'have a go';
- **active learning** - children concentrate and keep on trying if they encounter difficulties, and enjoy achievements; and
- **creating and thinking critically** - children have and develop their own ideas, make links between ideas, and develop strategies for doing things.

1.11 Each child must be assigned a key person[5] (a safeguarding and welfare requirement - see paragraph 3.26). Providers must inform parents and/or carers of the name of the key person, and explain their role, when a child starts attending a setting. The key person must help ensure that every child's learning and care is tailored to meet their individual needs. The key person must seek to engage and support parents and/or carers in guiding their child's development at home. They should also help families engage with more specialist support if appropriate.

1.12 A quality learning experience for children requires a quality workforce. A well qualified, skilled staff strongly increases the potential of any individual setting to deliver the best possible outcomes for children. Requirements in relation to staff qualifications are outlined in Section 3. Providers should regularly consider the training and development needs of all staff members to ensure they offer a quality learning experience for children that continually improves.

1.13 The level of progress children should be expected to have attained by the end of the EYFS is defined by the early learning goals set out below.

The early learning goals

The prime areas

Communication and language

Listening and attention: children listen attentively in a range of situations. They listen to stories, accurately anticipating key events and respond to what they hear with relevant comments, questions or actions. They give their attention to what others say and respond appropriately, while engaged in another activity.

Understanding: children follow instructions involving several ideas or actions. They answer 'how' and 'why' questions about their experiences and in response to stories or events.

Speaking: children express themselves effectively, showing awareness of listeners' needs. They use past, present and future forms accurately when talking about events that have happened or are to happen in the future. They develop their own narratives and explanations by connecting ideas or events.

Physical development

Moving and handling: children show good control and co-ordination in large and small movements. They move confidently in a range of ways, safely negotiating space. They handle equipment and tools effectively, including pencils for writing.

Health and self-care: children know the importance for good health of physical exercise, and a healthy diet, and talk about ways to keep healthy and safe. They manage their own basic hygiene and personal needs successfully, including dressing and going to the toilet independently.

Personal, social and emotional development

Self-confidence and self-awareness: children are confident to try new activities, and say why they like some activities more than others. They are confident to speak in a familiar group, will talk about their ideas, and will choose the resources they need for their chosen activities. They say when they do or don't need help.

Managing feelings and behaviour: children talk about how they and others show feelings, talk about their own and others' behaviour, and its consequences, and know that some behaviour is unacceptable. They work as part of a group or class, and understand and follow the rules. They adjust their behaviour to different situations, and take changes of routine in their stride.

Making relationships: children play co-operatively, taking turns with others. They take account of one another's ideas about how to organise their activity. They show sensitivity to others' needs and feelings, and form positive relationships with adults and other children.

The specific areas

Literacy

Reading: children read and understand simple sentences. They use phonic knowledge to decode regular words and read them aloud accurately. They also read some common irregular words. They demonstrate understanding when talking with others about what they have read.

Writing: children use their phonic knowledge to write words in ways which match their spoken sounds. They also write some irregular common words. They write simple sentences which can be read by themselves and others. Some words are spelt correctly and others are phonetically plausible.

[5] In childminding settings, the key person is the childminder.

Mathematics

Numbers: children count reliably with numbers from 1 to 20, place them in order and say which number is one more or one less than a given number. Using quantities and objects, they add and subtract two single-digit numbers and count on or back to find the answer. They solve problems, including doubling, halving and sharing.

Shape, space and measures: children use everyday language to talk about size, weight, capacity, position, distance, time and money to compare quantities and objects and to solve problems. They recognise, create and describe patterns. They explore characteristics of everyday objects and shapes and use mathematical language to describe them.

Understanding the world

People and communities: children talk about past and present events in their own lives and in the lives of family members. They know that other children don't always enjoy the same things, and are sensitive to this. They know about similarities and differences between themselves and others, and among families, communities and traditions.

The world: children know about similarities and differences in relation to places, objects, materials and living things. They talk about the features of their own immediate environment and how environments might vary from one another. They make observations of animals and plants and explain why some things occur, and talk about changes.

Technology: children recognise that a range of technology is used in places such as homes and schools. They select and use technology for particular purposes.

Expressive arts and design

Exploring and using media and materials: children sing songs, make music and dance, and experiment with ways of changing them. They safely use and explore a variety of materials, tools and techniques, experimenting with colour, design, texture, form and function.

Being imaginative: children use what they have learnt about media and materials in original ways, thinking about uses and purposes. They represent their own ideas, thoughts and feelings through design and technology, art, music, dance, role-play and stories.

Section 2 – Assessment

2.1 Assessment plays an important part in helping parents, carers and practitioners to recognise children's progress, understand their needs, and to plan activities and support. Ongoing assessment (also known as formative assessment) is an integral part of the learning and development process. It involves practitioners observing children to understand their level of achievement, interests and learning styles, and to then shape learning experiences for each child reflecting those observations. In their interactions with children, practitioners should respond to their own day-to-day observations about children's progress, and observations that parents and carers share.

2.2 Assessment should not entail prolonged breaks from interaction with children, nor require excessive paperwork. Paperwork should be limited to that which is absolutely necessary to promote children's successful learning and development. Parents and/or carers should be kept up-to-date with their child's progress and development. Practitioners should address any learning and development needs in partnership with parents and/or carers, and any relevant professionals.

Progress check at age two

2.3 When a child is aged between two and three, practitioners must review their progress, and provide parents and/or carers with a short written summary of their child's development in the prime areas. This progress check must identify the child's strengths, and any areas where the child's progress is less than expected. If there are significant emerging concerns, or an identified special educational need or disability, practitioners should develop a targeted plan to support the child's future learning and development involving other professionals (for example, the provider's Special Educational Needs Co-ordinator) as appropriate.

2.4 Beyond the prime areas, it is for practitioners to decide what the written summary should include, reflecting the development level and needs of the individual child. The summary must highlight: areas in which a child is progressing well; areas in which some additional support might be needed; and focus particularly on any areas where there is a concern that a child may have a developmental delay (which may indicate a special educational need or disability). It must describe the activities and strategies the provider intends to adopt to address any issues or concerns. If a child moves settings between the ages of two and three it is expected that the progress check would usually be undertaken by the setting where the child has spent most time.

2.5 Practitioners must discuss with parents and/or carers how the summary of development can be used to support learning at home. Practitioners should encourage parents and/or carers to share information from the progress check with other relevant professionals, including their health visitor, and/or a teacher (if a child moves to school-based provision at age three). Practitioners must agree with parents and/or carers when will be the most useful point to provide a summary. It should be provided in time to inform the Healthy Child Programme health and development review at age two whenever possible (when health visitors gather information on a child's health and development, allowing them to identify any developmental delay and any particular support from which they think the child/family might benefit). Taking account of information from the progress check (which reflects ongoing, regular observation of children's development) should help ensure that health visitors can identify children's needs accurately and fully at the health review. Providers must have the consent of parents and/or carers to share information directly with other relevant professionals, if they consider this would be helpful.

Assessment at the end of the EYFS – the Early Years Foundation Stage Profile (EYFSP)

2.6 In the final term of the year in which the child reaches age five, and no later than 30 June in that term, the EYFS Profile must be completed for each child. The Profile provides parents and carers, practitioners and teachers with a well-rounded picture of a child's knowledge, understanding and abilities, their progress against expected levels, and their readiness for Year 1. The Profile must reflect: ongoing observation; all relevant records held by the setting; discussions with parents and carers, and any other adults whom the teacher, parent or carer judges can offer a useful contribution.

2.7 Each child's level of development must be assessed against the early learning goals (see Section 1). Practitioners must indicate whether children are meeting expected levels of development, or if they are exceeding expected levels, or not yet reaching expected levels

('emerging'). This is the EYFS Profile.

2.8 Year 1 teachers must be given a copy of the Profile report together with a short commentary on each child's skills and abilities in relation to the three key characteristics of effective learning (see paragraph 1.10). These should inform a dialogue between Reception and Year 1 teachers about each child's stage of development and learning needs and assist with the planning of activities in Year 1.

2.9 Schools[6] must share the results of the Profile with parents and/or carers, and explain to them when and how they can discuss the Profile with the teacher[7] who completed it. For children attending more than one setting, the Profile must be completed by the school where the child spends most time. If a child moves to a new school during the academic year, the original school must send their assessment of the child's level of development against the early learning goals to the relevant school within 15 days of receiving a request. If a child moves during the summer term, relevant providers must agree which of them will complete the Profile.

2.10 The Profile must be completed for all children, including those with special educational needs or disabilities. Reasonable adjustments to the assessment process for children with special educational needs and disabilities must be made as appropriate. Providers should consider whether they may need to seek specialist assistance to help with this. Children will have differing levels of skills and abilities across the Profile and it is important that there is a full assessment of all areas of their development, to inform plans for future activities and to identify any additional support needs.
Information to be provided to the local authority

2.11 Early years providers must report EYFS Profile results to local authorities, upon request[8]. Local authorities are under a duty to return this data to the relevant Government department. Providers must permit the relevant local authority to enter their premises to observe the completion of the EYFS Profile, and permit the relevant local authority to examine and take copies of documents and other articles relating to the Profile and assessments[9]. Providers must take part in all reasonable moderation activities specified by their local authority and provide the local authority with such information relating to the EYFS Profile and assessment as they may reasonably request.

---

[6] Or the relevant provider.

[7] Or other practitioner.

[8] Childcare (Provision of Information About Young Children) (England) Regulations 2009.

[9] The Early Years Foundation Stage (Learning and Development Requirements) Order 2007.

Section 3 –
The Safeguarding and Welfare Requirements Introduction

3.1 Children learn best when they are healthy, safe and secure, when their individual needs are met, and when they have positive relationships with the adults caring for them. The safeguarding and welfare requirements, specified in this section, are designed to help providers create high quality settings which are welcoming, safe and stimulating, and where children are able to enjoy learning and grow in confidence.

3.2 Providers must take all necessary steps to keep children safe and well. The requirements in this section explain what early years providers must do to: safeguard children; ensure the suitability of adults who have contact with children; promote good health; manage behaviour; and maintain records, policies and procedures.

3.3 Schools are not required to have separate policies to cover EYFS requirements provided the requirements are already met through an existing policy. Where providers other than childminders are required to have policies and procedures as specified below, these policies and procedures should be recorded in writing. Childminders are not required to have written policies and procedures. However, they must be able to explain their policies and procedures to parents, carers, and others (for example Ofsted inspectors) and ensure any assistants follow them.

Child Protection

3.4 Providers must be alert to any issues for concern in the child's life at home or elsewhere. Providers must have and implement a policy, and procedures, to safeguard children. These should be in line with the guidance and procedures of the relevant Local Safeguarding Children Board (LSCB). The safeguarding policy and procedures must include an explanation of the action to be taken in the event of an allegation being made against a member of staff, and cover the use of mobile phones and cameras in the setting.

3.5 A practitioner must be designated to take lead responsibility for safeguarding children in every setting. Childminders must take the lead responsibility themselves. The lead practitioner is responsible for liaison with local statutory children's services agencies, and with the LSCB. They must provide support, advice and guidance to any other staff on an ongoing basis, and on any specific safeguarding issue as required. The lead practitioner must attend a child protection training course[10] that enables them to identify, understand and respond appropriately to signs of possible abuse and neglect (as described at paragraph 3.6).

3.6 Providers must train all staff to understand their safeguarding policy and procedures, and ensure that all staff have up to date knowledge of safeguarding issues. Training made available by the provider must enable staff to identify signs of possible abuse and neglect at the earliest opportunity, and to respond in a timely and appropriate way. These may include:

- significant changes in children's behaviour;
- deterioration in children's general well-being;
- unexplained bruising, marks or signs of possible abuse or neglect;
- children's comments which give cause for concern;
- any reasons to suspect neglect or abuse outside the setting, for example in the child's home; and/or
- inappropriate behaviour displayed by other members of staff, or any other person working with the children. For example, inappropriate sexual comments; excessive one-to-one attention beyond the requirements of their usual role and responsibilities; or inappropriate sharing of images.

3.7 Providers must have regard to the Government's statutory guidance 'Working Together to Safeguard Children'. If providers have concerns about children's safety or welfare, they must notify agencies with statutory responsibilities without delay. This means the local children's social care services and, in emergencies, the police.

3.8 Registered providers must inform Ofsted of any allegations of serious harm or abuse by any person living, working, or looking after children at the premises (whether the allegations relate to harm or abuse committed on the premises or elsewhere). Registered providers must also notify Ofsted of the action taken in respect of the allegations. These notifications must be made as soon as is reasonably practicable, but at the latest within 14 days of the allegations being made. A registered provider who, without reasonable excuse, fails to comply with this requirement, commits an offence.

---

[10] Taking account of any advice from the LSCB or local authority on appropriate training courses.

Suitable People

3.9 Providers must ensure that people looking after children are suitable to fulfil the requirements of their roles. Providers must have effective systems in place to ensure that practitioners, and any other person who is likely to have regular contact with children (including those living or working on the premises), are suitable[11].

3.10 Ofsted is responsible for checking the suitability of childminders and of persons living or working on a childminder's premises, including obtaining enhanced criminal records checks and barred list checks. Providers other than childminders must obtain an enhanced criminal records disclosure in respect of every person aged 16 and over who[12]:

- works directly with children;
- lives on the premises on which the childcare is provided; and/or
- works on the premises on which the childcare is provided (unless they do not work on the part of the premises where the childcare takes place, or do not work there at times when children are present).

3.11 Providers must tell staff that they are expected to disclose any convictions, cautions, court orders, reprimands and warnings which may affect their suitability to work with children (whether received before or during their employment at the setting). Providers must not allow people whose suitability has not been checked, including through a criminal records check, to have unsupervised contact with children being cared for.

3.12 Providers other than childminders must record information about staff qualifications and the identity checks and vetting processes that have been completed (including the criminal records disclosure, reference number, the date a disclosure was obtained and details of who obtained it). For childminders the relevant information will be kept by Ofsted.

3.13 Providers must also meet their responsibilities under the Safeguarding Vulnerable Groups Act 2006.

Disqualification
(all registered providers)

3.14 In the event of the disqualification[13] of a registered provider, a person living in the same household as the registered provider, or a person employed in that household, the provider must not continue as an early years provider – nor be directly concerned in the management of such provision. Where an employer becomes aware of relevant information which may lead to disqualification of an employee, the provider must take appropriate action to ensure the safety of children. In the event of disqualification of a person employed in early years provision, the provider must not continue to employ that person[14].

3.15 The provider must give Ofsted the following information when relevant:

- details of any order, determination, conviction, or other ground for disqualification from registration under regulations made under section 75 of the Childcare Act 2006;
- the date of the order, determination or conviction, or the date when the other ground for disqualification arose;
- the body or court which made the order, determination or conviction, and the sentence (if any) imposed; and
- a certified copy of the relevant order (in relation to an order or conviction).

3.16 The information must be provided to Ofsted as soon as reasonably practicable, but at the latest within 14 days of the date the provider became aware of the information or ought reasonably to have become aware of it if they had made reasonable enquiries.

---

[11] To allow Ofsted to make these checks, childminders are required to supply information to Ofsted, as set out in Schedule 1, Part 2 of the Childcare (Early Years Register) Regulations 2008, amended by the Childcare (Early Years Register) (Amendment) Regulations 2012. The requirements relating to people who live and work on childminder premises are in Schedule 1, Part 1.

[12] The requirement for a criminal records check will be deemed to have been met in respect of all people living or working in childcare settings, whose suitability was checked by Ofsted or their local authority before October 2005.

[13] In accordance with regulations made under Section 75 of the Childcare Act 2006.

[14] Under Section 76 of the Childcare Act 2006. In certain circumstances Ofsted may consider a waiver of the disqualification in line with the relevant legislation.

Staff taking medication/ other substances

3.17 Practitioners must not be under the influence of alcohol or any other substance which may affect their ability to care for children. If practitioners are taking medication which may affect their ability to care for children, those practitioners should seek medical advice. Providers must ensure that those practitioners only work directly with children if medical advice confirms that the medication is unlikely to impair that staff member's ability to look after children properly. Staff medication on the premises must be securely stored, and out of reach of children, at all times.

Staff qualifications, training, support and skills

3.18 The daily experience of children in early years settings and the overall quality of provision depends on all practitioners having appropriate qualifications, training, skills and knowledge and a clear understanding of their roles and responsibilities. Providers must ensure that all staff receive induction training to help them understand their roles and responsibilities. Induction training must include information about emergency evacuation procedures, safeguarding, child protection, the provider's equality policy, and health and safety issues.

3.19 Providers must put appropriate arrangements in place for the supervision of staff who have contact with children and families. Effective supervision provides support, coaching and training for the practitioner and promotes the interests of children. Supervision should foster a culture of mutual support, teamwork and continuous improvement which encourages the confidential discussion of sensitive issues.

3.20 Supervision should provide opportunities for staff to:
* discuss any issues – particularly concerning children's development or well-being;
* identify solutions to address issues as they arise; and
* receive coaching to improve their personal effectiveness.

3.21 In group settings, the manager must hold at least a full and relevant[15] level 3 qualification and at least half of all other staff must hold at least a full and relevant level 2 qualification. The manager should have at least two years' experience of working in an early years setting, or have at least two years' other suitable experience. The provider must ensure there is a named deputy who, in their judgement, is cap able and qualified to take charge in the manager's absence.

3.22 Providers should ensure that regular staff appraisals are carried out to identify any training needs, and secure opportunities for continued professional development for staff. Providers should support their staff to improve their qualification levels wherever possible. For staff without a relevant qualification, providers should consider supporting them to obtain a relevant level 2 qualification.

3.23 Childminders must have completed a local authority approved training course which helps them understand and implement the EYFS before they can register with Ofsted. Childminders are accountable for the quality of the work of any assistants, and must be satisfied that assistants are competent in the areas of work they undertake.

3.24 At least one person who has a current paediatric first aid certificate must be on the premises at all times when children are present, and must accompany children on outings. First aid training must be local authority approved and be relevant for workers caring for young children. Childminders, and any assistant who might be in sole charge of the children for any period of time, must hold a current paediatric first aid certificate.

3.25 Providers must ensure that staff have sufficient understanding and use of English to ensure the well-being of children in their care. For example, settings must be in a position to keep records in English, to liaise with other agencies in English, to summon emergency help, and to understand instructions such as those for the safety of medicines or food hygiene.

Key person

3.26 Each child must be assigned a key person. Their role is to help ensure that every child's care is tailored to meet their individual needs (in accordance with paragraph 1.11), to help the child become familiar with the setting, offer a settled relationship for the child and build a relationship with their parents.

15 As defined by the Teaching Agency.

Staff: child ratios

3.27 Staffing arrangements must meet the needs of all children and ensure their safety. Providers must ensure that children are adequately supervised and decide how to deploy staff to ensure children's needs are met. Providers must inform parents and/or carers about staff deployment, and, when relevant and practical, aim to involve them in these decisions. Children must usually be within sight and hearing of staff and always within sight or hearing.

3.28 Only those aged 17 or over may be included in ratios (and staff under 17 should be supervised at all times). Students on long term placements and volunteers (aged 17 or over) may be included if the provider is satisfied that they are competent and responsible.

3.29 The ratio and qualification requirements below apply to the total number of staff available to work directly with children[16]. For group settings providing overnight care, the relevant ratios continue to apply and at least one member of staff must be awake at all times. Exceptionally, and where the quality of care and safety and security of children is maintained, exceptions to the ratios may be made.

3.30 For children aged under two:
- there must be at least one member of staff for every three children;
- at least one member of staff must hold a full and relevant level 3 qualification, and must be suitably experienced in working with children under two;
- at least half of all other staff must hold a full and relevant level 2 qualification;
- at least half of all staff must have received training that specifically addresses the care of babies; and
- where there is an under two-year-olds' room, the member of staff in charge of that room must, in the judgement of the provider, have suitable experience of working with under twos.

3.31 For children aged two:
- there must be at least one member of staff for every four children;
- at least one member of staff must hold a full and relevant level 3 qualification; and
- at least half of all other staff must hold a full and relevant level 2 qualification.

3.32 For children aged three and over in registered early years provision operating between 8 am and 4pm where a person with Qualified Teacher Status, Early Years Professional Status or another suitable level 6 qualification (which is full and relevant) is working directly with the children:
- there must be at least one member of staff for every 13 children; and
- at least one other member of staff must hold a full and relevant level 3 qualification.

3.33 For children aged three and over at any time in registered early years provision operating outside the hours of 8 am and 4 pm, and between the hours of 8 am and 4 pm when a person with Qualified Teacher Status, Early Years Professional Status or another full and relevant level 6 qualification, is not working directly with the children:
- there must be at least one member of staff for every eight children;
- at least one member of staff must hold a full and relevant level 3 qualification;
- at least half of all other staff must hold a full and relevant level 2 qualification.

3.34 For children aged three and over in independent schools, where a person with Qualified Teacher Status, Early Years Professional Status or another full and relevant level 6 qualification, an instructor[17], or a suitably qualified overseas trained teacher, is working directly with the children:
- for classes where the majority of children will reach the age of 5 or older within the school year, there must be at least one member of staff for every 30 children;
- for all other classes there must be at least one member of staff for every 13 children; and
- at least one other member of staff must hold a full and relevant level 3 qualification.

3.35 For children aged three and over in independent schools, where there is no person with Qualified Teacher Status, Early Years Professional Status or another suitable level 6 qualifications, no instructor, and no suitably qualified overseas trained teacher, working directly with the children:
- there must be at least one member of staff for every eight children;
- at least one member of staff must hold a full and relevant level 3 qualification; and

[16] Ofsted may determine that providers must observe a higher staff:child ratio than outlined here to ensure the safety and welfare of children.

[17] An instructor is a person at the school who provides education which consists of instruction in any art or skill, or in any subject or group of subjects, in circumstances where:

(a) special qualifications or experience or both are required for such instruction, and

(b) the person or body of persons responsible for the management of the school is satisfied as to the qualifications or experience (or both) of the person providing education.

- at least half of all other staff must hold a full and relevant level 2 qualification.

3.36 For children aged three and over in maintained nursery schools and nursery classes in maintained schools (except for children in reception classes):

- there must be at least one member of staff for every 13 children;
- at least one member of staff must be a school teacher as defined by Section 122 of the Education Act 2002 and the Education (School Teachers' Qualifications) (England) Regulations 2003; and
- at least one other member of staff must hold a full and relevant level 3 qualification.

3.37 Reception classes in maintained schools are subject to infant class size legislation. The School Standards and Framework Act 1998 (as amended by the Education Act 2002) limits the size of infant classes to 30 pupils per school teacher[18]. 'School teachers' do not include teaching assistants, higher level teaching assistants or other support staff. Consequently, in a normal teaching session, a school must employ sufficient school teachers to enable it to teach its infant classes in groups of no more than 30 per school teacher[19].

3.38 Some schools may choose to mix their reception classes with groups of younger children, in which case they must determine ratios within mixed groups, guided by all relevant ratio requirements and by the needs of individual children within the group. In exercising this discretion, the school must comply with the statutory requirements relating to the education of children of compulsory school age and infant class sizes. Schools' partner providers must meet the relevant ratio requirements for their provision.

Childminders

3.39 At any one time, childminders may care for a maximum of six children under the age of eight[20]. Of these six children, a maximum of three may be young children[21], and there should only be one child under the age of one. Any care provided for older children must not adversely affect the care of children receiving early years provision.

3.40 If a childminder can demonstrate to parents and/or carers and inspectors, that the individual needs of all the children are being met, then exceptions to the usual ratios can be made when childminders are caring for sibling babies, or when caring for their own baby. If children aged four and five only attend the childminding setting before and/or after a normal school day, and/or during school holidays, they may be cared for at the same time as three other young children. But in all circumstances, the total number of children under the age of eight being cared for must not exceed six.

3.41 If a childminder employs an assistant or works with another childminder, each childminder (or assistant) may care for the number of children permitted by the ratios specified above[22]. Children may be left in the sole care of childminders' assistants for 2 hours at most in a single day[23]. Childminders must obtain parents and/or carers' permission to leave children with an assistant, including for very short periods of time. For childminders providing overnight care, the ratios continue to apply and the childminder must always be able to hear the children (this may be via a monitor).

Health

Medicines

3.42 The provider must promote the good health of children attending the setting. They must have a procedure, discussed with parents and/or carers, for responding to children who are ill or infectious, take necessary steps to prevent the spread of infection, and take appropriate action if children are ill.

3.43 Providers must have and implement a policy, and procedures, for administering medicines. It must include systems for obtaining information about a child's needs for medicines, and for keeping this information up-to-date. Training must be provided for staff where the administration of medicine requires medical or technical knowledge. Medicines must not usually be administered unless they have been prescribed for a child by a doctor, dentist, nurse or pharmacist (medicines containing aspirin should only be given if prescribed by a doctor).

---

[18] As defined by Section 122 of the Education Act 2002 and the Education (School Teachers' Qualifications) (England) Regulations 2003.

[19] Where children in nursery classes and reception classes attend school for longer than the school day or in the school holidays, in provision run directly by the governing body or the proprietor, with no teacher present, a ratio of one member of staff to every eight children can be applied if at least one member of staff holds a full and relevant level 3 qualification, and at least half of all other staff hold a full and relevant level 2 qualification.

[20] The numbers include the childminder's own children or any other children for whom they are responsible – for example, children who the childminder is fostering.

[21] A child is a young child up until 1st September following his or her fifth birthday.

[22] Subject to any restrictions imposed by Ofsted on registration.

[23] The Childcare (Exemptions from Registration) Order 2008 specifies that where provision is made for a particular child for two hours or less a day, the carer is exempt from registration as a childminder.

3.44 Medicine (both prescription and non-prescription) must only be administered to a child where written permission for that particular medicine has been obtained from the child's parent and/or carer. Providers must keep a written record each time a medicine is administered to a child, and inform the child's parents and/or carers on the same day, or as soon as reasonably practicable.

Food and drink

3.45 Where children are provided with meals, snacks and drinks, they must be healthy, balanced and nutritious. Before a child is admitted to the setting the provider must also obtain information about any special dietary requirements, preferences and food allergies that the child has, and any special health requirements. Fresh drinking water must be available and accessible at all times. Providers must record and act on information from parents and carers about a child's dietary needs.

3.46 There must be an area which is adequately equipped to provide healthy meals, snacks and drinks for children as necessary. There must be suitable facilities for the hygienic preparation of food for children, if necessary including suitable sterilisation equipment for babies' food. Providers must be confident that those responsible for preparing and handling food are competent to do so. In group provision, all staff involved in preparing and handling food must receive training in food hygiene.

3.47 Registered providers must notify Ofsted of any food poisoning affecting two or more children looked after on the premises. Notification must be made as soon as is reasonably practicable, but in any event within 14 days of the incident. A registered provider, who, without reasonable excuse, fails to comply with this requirement, commits an offence.

Accident or injury

3.48 Providers must ensure there is a first aid box accessible at all times with appropriate content for use with children. Providers must keep a written record of accidents or injuries and first aid treatment. Providers must inform parents and/or carers of any accident or injury sustained by the child on the same day, or as soon as reasonably practicable, of any first aid treatment given.

3.49 Registered providers must notify Ofsted of any serious accident, illness or injury to, or death of, any child while in their care, and of the action taken. Notification must be made as soon as is reasonably practicable, but in any event within 14 days of the incident occurring. A registered provider, who, without reasonable excuse, fails to comply with this requirement, commits an offence. Providers must notify local child protection agencies of any serious accident or injury to, or the death of, any child while in their care, and must act on any advice from those agencies.

Managing behaviour

3.50 Providers must have and implement a behaviour management policy, and procedures. A named practitioner should be responsible for behaviour management in every setting. They must have the necessary skills to advise other staff on behaviour issues and to access expert advice if necessary. In a childminding setting, the childminder is responsible for behaviour management.

3.51 Providers must not give corporal punishment to a child. Providers must take all reasonable steps to ensure that corporal punishment is not given by any person who cares for or is in regular contact with a child, or by any person living or working in the premises where care is provided. Any early years provider who fails to meet these requirements commits an offence. A person will not be taken to have used corporal punishment (and therefore will not have committed an offence), where physical intervention[24] was taken for the purposes of averting immediate danger of personal injury to any person (including the child) or to manage a child's behaviour if absolutely necessary. Providers, including childminders, must keep a record of any occasion where physical intervention is used, and parents and/or carers must be informed on the same day, or as soon as reasonably practicable.

3.52 Providers must not threaten corporal punishment, and must not use or threaten any punishment which could adversely affect a child's well-being.

---

[24] Physical intervention is where practitioners use reasonable force to prevent children from injuring themselves or others or damaging property.

Safety and suitability of premises, environment and equipment

Safety

3.53 Providers must ensure that their premises, including outdoor spaces, are fit for purpose. Spaces, furniture, equipment and toys, must be safe for children to use and premises must be secure. Providers must keep premises and equipment clean, and be aware of, and comply with, requirements of health and safety legislation (including hygiene requirements). Providers must have, and implement, a health and safety policy, and procedures, which cover identifying, reporting and dealing with accidents, hazards and faulty equipment.

3.54 Providers must take reasonable steps to ensure the safety of children, staff and others on the premises in the case of fire or any other emergency, and must have an emergency evacuation procedure. Providers must have appropriate fire detection and control equipment (for example, fire alarms, smoke detectors, and fire extinguishers) which is in working order. Fire exits must be clearly identifiable, and fire doors must be free of obstruction and easily opened from the inside.

Smoking

3.55 Providers must have a no smoking policy, and must prevent smoking in a room, or outside play area, when children are present or about to be present.

Premises

3.56 The premises and equipment must be organised in a way that meets the needs of children. In registered provision, providers must meet the following indoor space requirements[25]:

- Children under two years: 3.5 m2 per child.
- Two year olds: 2.5 m2 per child.
- Children aged three to five years: 2.3 m2 per child.

3.57 The provider must ensure that, so far as is reasonable, the facilities, equipment and access to the premises are suitable for children with disabilities. Providers must provide access to an outdoor play area or, if that is not possible, ensure that outdoor activities are planned and taken on a daily basis (unless circumstances make this inappropriate, for example unsafe weather conditions).

3.58 Provision must be made (space or partitioned area) for children who wish to relax, play quietly or sleep, equipped with appropriate furniture. Sleeping children must be frequently checked. Except in childminding settings, there should be a separate baby room for children under the age of two. However, providers must ensure that children in a baby room have contact with older children and are moved into the older age group when appropriate.

3.59 Providers must ensure there is an adequate number of toilets and hand basins available (usually one toilet and one hand basin for every ten children over the age of two). Except in childminding settings, there should usually be separate toilet facilities for adults. Providers must ensure there are suitable hygienic changing facilities for changing any children who are in nappies and providers should ensure that an adequate supply of clean bedding, towels, spare clothes and any other necessary items is always available.

3.60 Providers must also ensure that there is an area where staff may talk to parents and/or carers confidentially, as well as an area in group settings for staff to take breaks away from areas being used by children.

3.61 Providers must only release children into the care of individuals who have been notified to the provider by the parent, and must ensure that children do not leave the premises unsupervised. Providers must take all reasonable steps to prevent unauthorised persons entering the premises, and have an agreed procedure for checking the identity of visitors. Providers must consider what additional measures are necessary when children stay overnight.

3.62 Providers must carry public liability insurance.

Risk assessment

3.63 Providers must have a clear and well-understood policy, and procedures, for assessing any risks to children's safety, and review risk assessments regularly. Providers must determine where it is helpful to make some written risk assessments in relation to specific issues, to inform staff practice, and to demonstrate how they are managing risks if asked by parents and/or carers or inspectors. Risk assessments should identify aspects of the environment that need to be checked on a regular basis, when and by whom those aspects will be checked, and how the risk will be removed or minimised.

---

[25] These calculations should be based on the net or useable areas of the rooms used by the children, not including storage areas, thoroughfares, dedicated staff areas, cloakrooms, utility rooms, kitchens and toilets.

Outings

3.64 Children must be kept safe while on outings, and providers must obtain written parental permission for children to take part in outings. Providers must assess the risks or hazards which may arise for the children, and must identify the steps to be taken to remove, minimise and manage those risks and hazards. The assessment must include consideration of adult to child ratios. The risk assessment does not necessarily need to be in writing; this is for providers to judge.

3.65 Vehicles in which children are being transported, and the driver of those vehicles, must be adequately insured.

Equal opportunities

3.66 Providers must have and implement a policy, and procedures, to promote equality of opportunity for children in their care, including support for children with special educational needs or disabilities. The policy should cover: how the individual needs of all children will be met (including how those children who are disabled or have special educational needs, will be included, valued and supported, and how reasonable adjustments will be made for them); the name of the Special Educational Needs Co-ordinator (in group provision); arrangements for reviewing, monitoring and evaluating the effectiveness of inclusive practices that promote and value diversity and difference; how inappropriate attitudes and practices will be challenged; and how the provision will encourage children to value and respect others.

Information and records

3.67 Providers must maintain records and obtain and share information (with parents and carers, other professionals working with the child, and the police, social services and Ofsted as appropriate) to ensure the safe and efficient management of the setting, and to help ensure the needs of all children are met. Providers must enable a regular two-way flow of information with parents and/or carers, and between providers, if a child is attending more than one setting. If requested, providers should incorporate parents' and/or carers' comments into children's records.

3.68 Records must be easily accessible and available (with prior agreement from Ofsted, these may be kept securely off the premises). Confidential information and records about staff and children must be held securely and only accessible and available to those who have a right or professional need to see them. Providers must be aware of their responsibilities under the Data Protection Act (DPA) 1998 and where relevant the Freedom of Information Act 2000.

3.69 Providers must ensure that all staff understand the need to protect the privacy of the children in their care as well the legal requirements that exist to ensure that information relating to the child is handled in a way that ensures confidentiality. Parents and/or carers must be given access to all records about their child, provided that no relevant exemptions apply to their disclosure under the DPA[26].

3.70 Records relating to individual children must be retained for a reasonable period of time after they have left the provision.

Information about the child

3.71 Providers must record the following information for each child in their care: full name; date of birth; name and address of every parent and/or carer who is known to the provider (and information about any other person who has parental responsibility for the child); which parent(s) and/or carer(s) the child normally lives with; and emergency contact details for parents and/or carers.

Information for parents and carers

3.72 Providers must make the following information available to parents and/or carers:
- how the EYFS is being delivered in the setting, and how parents and/or carers can access more information (for example, via the DfE website);
- the range and type of activities and experiences provided for children, the daily routines of the setting, and how parents and carers can share learning at home;
- how the setting supports children with special educational needs and disabilities;

---

[26] The Data Protection Act 1998 (DPA) gives parents and carers the right to access information about their child that a provider holds. However, the DPA also sets out specific exemptions under which certain personal information may, under specific circumstances, be withheld from release. For example, a relevant professional will need to give careful consideration as to whether the disclosure of certain information about a child could cause harm either to the child or any other individual. It is therefore essential that all providers/staff in early years settings have an understanding of how data protection laws operate. Further guidance can be found on the website of the Information Commissioner's Office at: http://www.ico.gov.uk/for_organisations/data_protection.aspx .

- food and drinks provided for children;
- details of the provider's policies and procedures (all providers except childminders must make copies available on request) including the procedure to be followed in the event of a parent and/or carer failing to collect a child at the appointed time, or in the event of a child going missing at, or away from, the setting; and
- staffing in the setting; the name of their child's key person and their role; and a telephone number for parents and/or carers to contact in an emergency.

Complaints

3.73 Providers must put in place a written procedure for dealing with concerns and complaints from parents and/or carers, and must keep a written record of any complaints, and their outcome. Childminders are not required to have a written procedure for handling complaints, but they must keep a record of any complaints they receive and their outcome. All providers must investigate written complaints relating to their fulfillment of the EYFS requirements and notify complainants of the outcome of the investigation within 28 days of having received the complaint. The record of complaints must be made available to Ofsted on request.

3.74 Providers must make available to parents and/or carers details about how to contact Ofsted, if they believe the provider is not meeting the EYFS requirements. If providers become aware that they are to be inspected, they must notify parents and/or carers. After an inspection, providers must supply a copy of the report to parents and/or carers of children attending on a regular basis.

Information about the provider

3.75 Providers must hold the following documentation:
- name, home address and telephone number of the provider and any other person living or employed on the premises (this requirement does not apply to childminders);
- name, home address and telephone number of anyone else who will regularly be in unsupervised contact with the children attending the early years provision;
- a daily record of the names of the children being cared for on the premises, their hours of attendance and the names of each child's key person; and

- their certificate of registration (which must be displayed at the setting and shown to parents and/or carers on request).
- Changes that must be notified to Ofsted

3.76 All registered early years providers must notify Ofsted of:
- any change in the address of the premises; to the premises which may affect the space available to children and the quality of childcare available to them; in the name or address of the provider, or the provider's other contact information; to the person who is managing the early years provision; or in the persons aged 16 years or older living or working on childminding premises;[27]
- any proposal to change the hours during which childcare is provided; or to provide overnight care;
- any significant event which is likely to affect the suitability of the early years provider or any person who cares for, or is in regular contact with, children on the premises to look after children;
- where the early years provision is provided by a company, any change in the name or registered number of the company;
- where the early years provision is provided by a charity, any change in the name or registration number of the charity;
- where the childcare is provided by a partnership, body corporate or unincorporated association, any change to the 'nominated individual'; and
- where the childcare is provided by a partnership, body corporate or unincorporated association whose sole or main purpose is the provision of childcare, any change to the individuals who are partners in, or a director, secretary or other officer or members of its governing body.

3.77 Where providers are required to notify Ofsted about a change of person except for managers, as specified in paragraph 3.76 above, providers must give Ofsted the new person's name, any former names or aliases, date of birth, and home address. If there is a change of manager, providers must notify Ofsted that a new manager has been appointed. Where it is reasonably practicable to do so, notification must be made in advance. In other cases, notification must be made as soon as is reasonably practicable, but always within 14 days. A registered provider who, without reasonable excuse, fails to comply with these requirements commits an offence.

[27] A person is not considered to be working on the premises if none of their work is done in the part of the premises in which children are cared for, or if they do not work on the premises at times when children are there.